FATHER AND CHILD

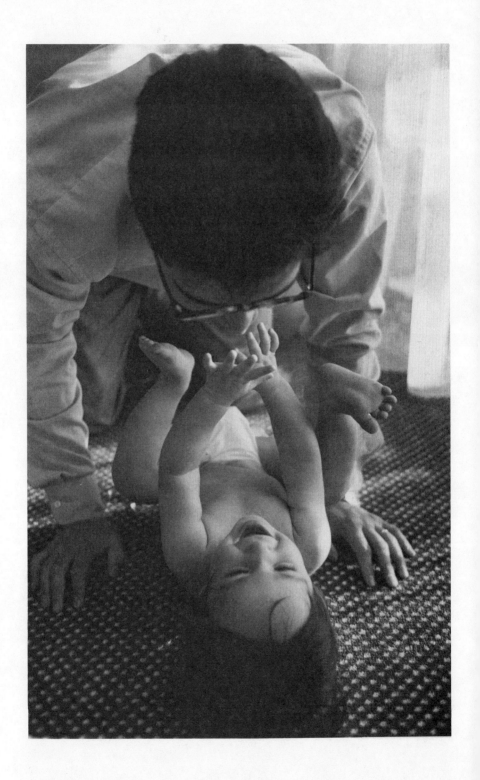

FATHER
AND
CHILD

Practical Advice for Today's Dad

Robert Ostermann
Christopher Spurrell
and
Carolyn T. Chubet

Longmeadow Press

**PREPARED FOR LONGMEADOW PRESS BY
IRENA CHALMERS BOOKS, INC.**

Photography by Elizabeth Crews
Managing Editor: Jean Atcheson
Art Direction & Design: Helene Berinsky
Typesetting: ComCom, Allentown, Pennsylvania

This publication is designed to provide accurate and authoritative information regarding the subject matter covered. This text is not meant to be exhaustive on the
information presented herein. Neither the publisher nor the author is engaged in
providing professional services or medical advice. Should assistance be desired, the
services of a competent professional should be sought.

FATHER AND CHILD

A compilation of materials originally appearing in *Fathering, Your Growing Baby,
Raising a Happy Baby* and excerpts from *Your Baby's Health and Safety*—all copy-
right © 1988 by Carolyn T. Chubet—in the No Nonsense Parenting Guide™ series.

ISBN 0-681-41033-7

Printed in the United States of America

0 9 8 7 6 5 4 3 2 1

For Deirdre, Liam, Darina, Denise and
Shaw; for Cailyn and Katie; for John,
Charlie—and Tom

Our thanks to Malcolm M. Brown, M.D., of the Sharon, Connecticut, Pediatric Association, and to Judy Kay Morris, R.N., Certified Nurse-Midwife with the Sharon, Connecticut, Ob-Gyn Associates, for their insightful comments on the subject of fathering and babies.

Contents

PART III: RAISING A HAPPY BABY

PART IV: TAKING CARE OF YOUR BABY'S HEALTH

Foreword

When you discover that you're going to be a father, you may feel tremendously elated. Life suddenly takes on new meaning. A surging sense of accomplishment and purpose makes you feel almost superhuman, ready to leap tall buildings at a single bound. But you may also feel afraid—this major change in your life brings with it a load of responsibilities and the worries that inevitably go along with them. You may feel somewhat overwhelmed at first. Don't worry—this is just the first step in taking on the role of father. It's a gradual evolution that lasts a lifetime.

Fatherhood is what you make it. Biologically, you have already done the only job you absolutely *have* to do! You *could* leave your wife to handle the rest of the process. Some men do. Obviously, you're not one of them, or you wouldn't be reading this book. You are intrigued with fathering and want to explore its full range of possibilities. By doing so, you join a vanguard of men who commit themselves profoundly to nurturing the babies they have made—by sharing in the wondrous process of pregnancy and birth, by learning how babies grow from infants into toddlers, by understanding and supporting the development of each tiny child int an absolutely unique, individual human being.

In the past, in our culture (and many others), fathers took a back seat in the process of birth and early childhood parenting.

Social values and attitudes, behavioral patterns and self-image all reinforced the traditional role of fathers solely in economic terms. If you were a generous and dependable provider, you were a good father. You had measured up.

Beyond that, what was there? Fathers were just about invisible in the self-help articles and books, which focused on the mother-to-be. If you took these works seriously, men had no emotional connection with their partners that pregnancy might disrupt, and were expected to be immune to the turbulence following childbirth and the intrusion of a totally dependent human being into what had been a exclusive twosome. Fathers were little more than spectators at the drama of pregnancy, birth and beyond.

Also ignored was the possibility that being a father might enrich you, stretch your emotional range, breach the existing frontiers of your relationship with your wife and give you an exciting role in creating a new community: the family. Fortunately, that tradition is rapidly being replaced by a more generous one that puts fathers where they belong, at the very center of the parenting experience.

As you join other men who have discovered the joy and challenge of fathering, you will find that some of your responses to the experience and solutions to its problems may be different from those of your friends. Just as no two people are alike, no two families are alike. Don't judge yourself by the casual responses and opinions of others. They aren't *you* and can't truly know your situation.

Fathering offers few universal truths to follow. More often than not, you will find yourself swinging from branch to branch of "if, then" statements, moving from one decision point to the next. Good medical advice, careful thought and planning and a healthy dose of common sense will get you and your new family safely from point A to point B. There are no pat answers. The more flexible you can be, the easier and more rewarding the whole experience will be—for you, your wife and your baby.

We have written this book to help first-time fathers understand what is involved in nurturing a baby all the way from conception to the age of two. Exactly what part you decide to play in this process will depend on your personality, your partner and your family's circumstances. There is never just one "right" way to be a father—just the one that best suits *you*.

Because approximately equal numbers of boy and girl babies are born—fortunately for the human race—we refer to your baby as "he" or "she" in alternate chapters of this book.

PART I

BECOMING A FATHER

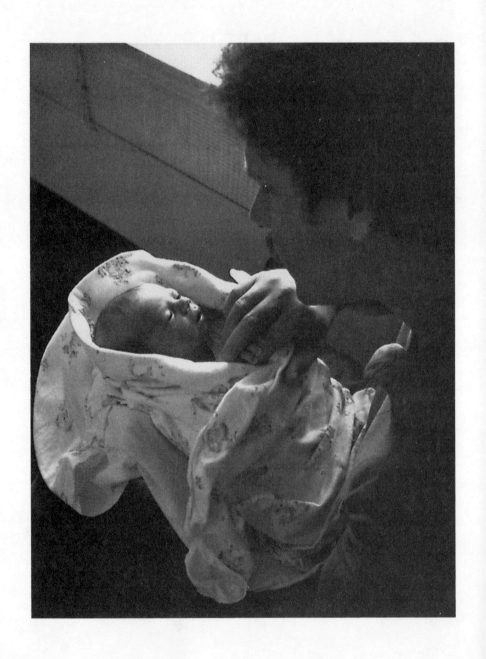

Becoming a father is a rite of passage that evolves over months and months. Traveling through each stage of the ritual—pregnancy, birth and nurturing your baby—adds a new dimension to your personality. The man you become will be able to handle any situation that fatherhood demands. As you take each hurdle cleanly, you build new confidence.

To help you on your way, we'll discuss in this section many of the principal joys and anxieties you will find yourself facing and suggest ways to handle some of the difficulties that lie ahead. We'll take the challenge of pregnancy, childbirth and parenting and break it down into manageable pieces. And we'll encourage you to share each step with your wife. If you and she work together, the intimate circle of your marriage will gradually expand. And when the time comes, you will both be ready to receive the baby with joy and gladness.

As you and your partner go through pregnancy together and into the unfolding experience of a family, it might also help to keep this maxim before you:

Don't be the kind of father others may think you ought to be. Be the kind of father *you* will be proud to be.

1

Pregnancy: A Time of Change

You have just learned that you are going to be a father, and in an instant your whole world has changed. Along with this exciting news came a new set of rules and roles. The part your wife plays is clearly defined: She carries the baby. Her immediate task is caring for her health and coping with the changes in her body. From Day One hormones are on the job, enabling the baby's proper development and often causing many of pregnancy's discomforts. For the next nine months she will nurture within her body this tiny life both of you have created, from a microdot of potential to a brand-new human being.

While your partner has the physical role in the pregnancy, you must both adjust to the change that is scrambling up your lives. *You*, the father-to-be, are psychologically pregnant. In these unsettled months, you are worried. What is happening to our relationship? What will happen to our relationship when the baby comes? Can we afford it? Should we have waited?

As time goes by, you will get used to the idea of having a baby. Your worries will fade, but don't expect them to disappear altogether. Doubts will linger until after the baby is born. Try to put them away. Remember that babies are born—and raised—successfully all the time. Your baby's future is not dependent on how much you worry! It is much better to spend your emotional energy on the step-by-step approach to fathering described here.

The baby growing in your wife's womb signals that some

changes lie ahead. Indeed, it is a clear new beginning. The months of pregnancy are a grace period, allowing new parents to settle in gradually. If you use the time wisely, you will be ready when the baby is. (If you are reading this book for the first time at the end of your partner's pregnancy, it is not too late to catch up.)

As you grow into parenthood, you naturally reorganize your priorities and your philosophy. While you are redefining the meaning of life, keep one priority from the old days on top: your relationship. It is vital that you keep the lines of communication open as you set your course as new parents. You will need huge reserves of patience and understanding as emotions fluctuate during pregnancy. Be prepared to be sometimes puzzled, hurt or angry.

ESTIMATING YOUR BABY'S DUE DATE

Your baby will be born approximately 40 weeks after conception. To calculate the estimated due date (EDD), you and your
wife will count back three months from the first day of her last
period and add seven days. Remember that this is only an
approximation. There is a two-week window before and after
that particular day.

You know how you feel. As much as you might try to imagine on your own what pregnancy is like, you won't be able to. That's why it is important to find out how *she* feels. Explore her experience now as her pregnancy advances, and later when she is home with the baby. Talk with her. Listen to her. Tell her how you feel. Chances are, you'll be closer to her than ever.

The Three Trimesters of Pregnancy

Your baby's rapid development is a major biological feat accomplished in a very short time. So much happens so fast that it almost seems like watching a time-lapse film of a flower bud coming into bloom. And, of course, it is all the more wonderful because it is your very own baby.

For both baby and mother the nine months of pregnancy fall naturally into three segments, or trimesters. Even though no two babies or pregnancies are alike, each three-month section has a flavor and characteristics all its own:

MONTHS 1 TO 3

Your baby: The first three months are critical for your baby. The baby's entire skeletal framework is formed with hands and feet, fingers and toes. Her face appears. Her heart starts beating and tiny muscles are flexing their might.

By the end of three months she's a mighty two inches long (remember, she started out about the size of the period at the end of this sentence). In this trimester, if something isn't right with the fetus, it may well spontaneously abort (the medical term for miscarriage). We'll discuss that in a later section.

Your wife: She is probably tired much of the time and may not have much energy. She may feel very sick at the sight of food. She may go to bed for the night ten minutes after she gets home from work. She will continue to feel this way until the placenta, which oversees the baby's development and is being formed during these first three months, can take over the work of the pregnancy. She's worried about miscarriage and won't feel relieved until this trimester is over.

MONTHS 4 TO 6

Your baby: Your baby develops her bone structure as preliminary cartilage turns into bone. Her brain develops and she begins to make her presence known—doing butterfly kicks and double back flips. She may even suck her thumb. By the end of six months she has grown two and a half times her length at three months. She is about 12 inches long and weighs more than a pound.

Your wife: This is the golden age. Her complexion glows. She is truly radiant. She regains a good deal of strength, as well as her appetite. Your baby is nestled in and the placenta takes charge.

```
┌─────────────────────────────────────────────────────────┐
│                                                         │
│        HOW MUCH A SAMPLE PREGNANCY WEIGHS                │
│                                                         │
│           Baby                        7.5 lbs.          │
│           Placenta                    2 lbs.            │
│           Amniotic fluid              2 lbs.            │
│           Maternal blood volume       4 lbs.            │
│           Uterus, breast tissue       4 lbs.            │
│           Extracellular fluid         4 lbs.            │
│           Maternal fat stores         2 lbs.            │
│                                                         │
│           Total                       25.5 lbs.         │
│                                                         │
└─────────────────────────────────────────────────────────┘
```

MONTHS 7 TO 9

Your baby: She gets some final touches, including important antibodies to help fight disease, and a protective covering for her skin. She puts on a final growth spurt, gaining a half pound to a full pound each week and growing a total of about eight more inches. As your baby grows, she has much less room to romp and your wife's abdomen will roll when she does. You may even see a lump pop up temporarily when she kicks.

If she is born in the middle of this trimester she'll have about a 90 percent chance of survival. A full-term baby averages about 20 inches in length and about 7.7 or 7.8 pounds.

Your wife: She is growing so heavy that moving around may be an effort for her. She begins to wish that the baby were already born. You both find it hard to wait for the birth.

Those Morning Blues . . . and Blahs

About half of all women experience the nausea of morning sickness in the first three months. For these women the smell or sight of food is unpleasant indeed. Despite the name, morning sickness doesn't happen only in the morning. Some women are hit later in the day, or are offended by certain foods and odors at any time.

HOW IT FEELS TO BE PREGNANT

Every pregnancy is different, but there are some common denominators to be aware of. The following is a list of physical changes her body is going through and some ways you can help her cope:

What Happens	Why	What You Can Do
Radical mood swings and weepy spells	Dramatic increase in hormonal activity	Give her your love and understanding.
Sore breasts	Hormonal activity preparing them for nursing	Avoid caressing or fondling them during lovemaking.
Stretched abdomen with organs becoming increasingly crowded	The baby's growth	Support her need for many small meals; help her avoid spicy foods and add fiber for good digestion.
Inability to sleep	Bad dreams, baby kicking, the frequent need to urinate	Massage her, encourage other relaxation techniques; give her the comfort of snuggling.
Heaviness and awkwardness in the third trimester	Increased size of the pregnancy; loosening of pelvic joints in preparation for childbirth	Don't insist that she dance with you or expect her to move around as she used to.

Morning sickness varies in intensity: Some women have trouble keeping anything down, while others need simply to be very particular about what they eat.

"I DON'T KNOW HOW TO COOK" MEALS

Don't think of asking her to cook. Do as much of the meal preparation as you can, and try to make meals as tempting for her as you can manage.

If you can't cook, this is the time to learn. To stem starvation while you learn, here's a short list of balanced meals that you can make. Don't worry if dinner looks like breakfast sometimes; breakfast foods are often comfort foods, just right for a fragile stomach. Use the list below for inspiration. A little of this, a little of that, and voilà, you've got a meal fit for a baby.

- Plain or vanilla yogurt in a bowl, topped with a crunchy bran cereal and raisins or other fruit.
- Peanut butter spread on one or two slices of whole wheat toast, topped with sliced bananas.
- Chef's salad: sliced deli turkey, ham and a mild cheese on a bed of shredded lettuce with a creamy bottled dressing (tomatoes and cucumbers may be added if desired). Tuna from a can or a hard-cooked egg may be substituted for the meats.
- Blender magic. Start with a pint of skimmed milk, add ¼ cup wheat germ or bran, 1–2 tablespoons honey, bananas or other favorite fruit. Whirl until thoroughly blended.

Remember: Bland foods are more appealing to a delicate stomach than rich, spicy or fried foods.

Cravings

Stories are legion about the crazy food longings of pregnant women: pickles and ice cream at midnight, applesauce laced with ketchup, salads with french fries. Such cravings probably belong more to folklore than to facts. Reality is much less exotic. Pregnant women usually tilt toward the starchy end of the table on the one hand and citrus fruits on the other.

Bizarre food can be limited; more important is to keep a runaway appetite in check and to ensure a nutritious diet. She

DAILY MENU: THE FOUR BASIC FOOD GROUPS

Your wife's medical team will give her a dietary menu to follow during pregnancy and she should follow it as closely as possible. The diet plan she receives will probably include:

Type	Main Benefits
1. Milk and milk products, including cheese, yogurt and cottage cheese, the lower in fat the better	Calcium to build your new baby's bones and other vital functions
2. Meats, chicken and fish, concentrating on the lower fat cuts, with any skin removed	Protein to build your baby's tissues
3. Vegetables and fruits, including the dark green and yellow vegetables, and citrus fruits as well as other kinds	Vitamins A, B and C for general health of mother and baby
4. Grains, breads and cereals, preferably the high-bran, whole wheat variety	B vitamins (see above) and fiber for good digestion

shouldn't eat double the amount of food because she is eating for two. She really needs only a few hundred extra calories (the amount she needs depends on her metabolism and the amount of exercise she gets).

Many doctors recommend that women should gain only about 25 pounds steadily and gradually throughout the pregnancy. For example, if your wife gained half a pound a week during the first 20 weeks and a pound a week during the last 20 weeks, she would gain 30 pounds. The theory is that excess weight tends to hang on stubbornly after pregnancy is over, and might delay your wife's return to her old self as soon as possible. However, some women gain much more weight than is generally recommended *and* are able to lose it all afterwards.

HEALTHY GUIDELINES FOR HER PREGNANCY

What	Why
No cigarettes (it would be best not to smoke around her either)	Dangers of miscarriage and premature delivery, low birthweight
Little or no alcohol	The dangers of moderate consumption to the fetus are not as yet well understood. Brain damage and other abnormalities are often the result of heavy drinking during pregnancy.
No recreational drugs, like marijuana and cocaine	Little is known about the effects on pregnancy and it is common sense to avoid taking risks with a baby's fragile life.
No prescription or *non*prescription drugs without consulting her doctor	Little is known about the effects of many medicines on pregnancy. Common medicines like aspirin and antihistamines should probably be avoided. Some antibiotics, tranquilizers and hormones are known to cause malformations.
Caffeine in moderation	Caffeine was long suspected to be dangerous in pregnancy, but recent findings discount the risk. Keep in mind, however, that caffeine (a) enters the fetal bloodstream and (b) may interfere with your wife's sleep.

You can play a significant role here by not indulging your taste for hamburgers, pastries and the empty calories of alcohol. Perhaps the fact that she probably should abstain from alcohol completely will inspire you to abstain as well. It is hard for her to be a saint when the devil is at her elbow.

PHYSICAL CHANGES, BODILY DISCOMFORTS

Your wife may complain of physical ailments during pregnancy. Sometimes all you can do is to listen with a sympathetic ear. Sometimes you can offer real relief.

Complaint	Possible Causes	Possible Remedies
Backache	Uterus exerting pressure on lower back; ligaments or joints loosening	Remind her to stand straight; offer her massage, a heating pad; remind her to sleep on her side, knees up
Constipation	Intestines blocked by uterus; bowel-needed water absorbed elsewhere; hormonal activity blocking digestion	See that she drinks extra water and eats bran and fiber, prunes; take a walk with her
Tiredness	Sedative power of progesterone; feature of early pregnancy before placenta takes over; natural feature of late pregnancy	Encourage her to listen to her body; suggest that she sleep and rest as much as possible; take another walk with her
Heartburn/ indigestion	Digestion slowed by hormonal activity; pressure from enlarged uterus	Help her avoid "trouble" foods; see that she eats small meals and sips carbonated fluids
Hemorrhoids	Constipation and straining; hormonal activity strains bowel movements, dilates rectal veins	Get her off her feet, with hips raised; offer an ice pack or medicated swabs

Complaint	Possible Causes	Possible Remedies
Muscle cramp/charley horse	Fatigue; calcium imbalance; sluggish circulation; not enough salt; pointing toes	Suggest a warm bath, give her a light massage; give her hurt muscle rapid massage; pull her foot toward her
Shooting pains	Pelvic ligaments, bones and nerves getting ready for baby	Remind her to try the Kegel exercise (when she squeezes her vaginal and rectal muscles together and then releases)
Swelling/edema	Fluid retention (the body becomes a giant sponge)	Watch salt in her diet; offer water (not soda); suggest she lie down on left side, with legs raised on a cushion
Varicose veins	Hormone activity in muscles; excessive weight gain; heredity	Suggest she lie down on left side, with feet up; remind her not to cross her legs; suggest that she wear support stockings; watch her weight
Dizzy spells	Brain suffers decrease in oxygen-rich blood, now diverted to uterus	Sit her down quickly, put her head to her knees and get her to take deep breaths; make sure she eats regularly

Sometimes the ravenous pregnant appetite can be traced to sources other than hunger. Problems of self-image and other insecurities can surface as "I want to eat . . . ." What she may be saying is: "I'm worried. I'm not attractive. I'm not loved." In fact, she is confronted with a direct choice between you and the refrigerator. Make it your business that she picks you.

TIP: If she has trouble with temptation, you need to set an extra-good example at home. *But* the goodies you eat at a business lunch or the mound of french fries that disappears every lunch hour at your desk are your business alone.

A Slower Social Whirl

Your social life may be much quieter now and you may have to be more selective about your social engagements. Say goodbye to spontaneity and hello to thoughtful planning. The invitations you accept or proffer must be tailored to your wife's energies and capabilities. This may not be easy for you, because *your* body isn't changing—your legs don't hurt, you don't hate crowded places or the sight of most food—but you need to do it all the same. (She may well agree to let you go on alone sometimes, but don't abuse this privilege. After a while, she'll resent it.)

If morning sickness is troubling her, and friends call to invite you over for dinner, you may want to tell them about the problem to save her the embarrassment of having to do so. Choose to accept only the most appealing invitations. Don't bunch up the parties back to back. Avoid stand-up cocktail parties. She will wilt, if not faint, in crowded, hot rooms. Later on, as her baby grows, she will not be able to tolerate standing for long periods.

Pregnancy Is Hard Work

Some women sail through pregnancy. Others don't. If your wife is having a difficult (though perfectly normal) pregnancy, she may not always be in a good mood. Hormonal activity and discomfort may make her ill-tempered at times and she won't necessarily keep her unhappiness to herself. Banish the myth that pregnancy is a wonderful time for her. Though she may have an easier time in subsequent pregnancies, this time it isn't much fun. If you make it clear to her that you understand that she has a hard job to do, one that *you* certainly wouldn't relish, you may find the storm clouds clearing a bit. You might even see a patch of blue.

Miscarriage

About one in five pregnancies ends in miscarriage. If early pregnancy ends abruptly, it usually means that there was a problem. Miscarriage is disappointing, but it does not prevent you from trying to get pregnant again.

Vaginal bleeding accompanied with cramps is an early sign of possible miscarriage. About a third of all women have some spotting during their pregnancy. Sometimes the bleeding is benign and the pregnancy goes to full term; at other times, the pregnancy ends within a day or two after the bleeding starts. If your wife experiences bleeding during pregnancy, notify your medical team as soon as possible, but don't be overly alarmed. She will probably be advised to rest and abstain from sexual activities.

If the bleeding stops, the pregnancy is likely to be successful: Full-term babies born after the pregnancy has been threatened by bleeding are just as likely to be normal as any other baby.

Sexual Love

Many couples who are pregnant for the first time find it difficult to adjust to changes in their sexual relationship. These changes interfere with your sexual access to each other and can prompt impatience, hurt and anger. So you should be absolutely clear about how the different stages of your wife's pregnancy may affect your sexual relationship with her. Know what you can do and when, and what to be careful about.

There is wide expert agreement that intercourse during pregnancy is okay and desirable. Except in particular circumstances,

THE SHAPE OF LOVE

You may be afraid that you will lose sexual desire for your wife as her belly and breasts swell. Some fathers report that they regarded their wives as more beautiful and more exciting when full with child than they ever imagined; others found their sex life put temporarily on hold. If your sex life all but disappears during pregnancy, it doesn't mean that you have stopped loving her, and hugs and kisses can go a long way toward keeping the pilot light of your relationship going.

Pregnant women are often self-conscious about their figures. She may feel fat and awkward. She may take offense if she even suspects you have lost your desire for her. Look for ways to give her pleasure, no matter how you feel. Tell her she's beautiful. Don't tease her. It may do irreparable harm.

And if you are afraid that she may never be sexually exciting to you again, look around you. Have you ever seen so many attractive young mothers walking with their toddlers? But remember that she may need time—and help—to rekindle sexual desire after the baby is born. (There are ways to help her regain her fire; see Chapter 5.)

---

sex during the first two trimesters of pregnancy is safe. There is some controversy about the third trimester, with liberal voices saying that if sex feels okay, it *is* okay. If you are uncertain, consult your doctor.

Be prepared for changes in the intensity of your sexual desire and hers as you proceed through the different stages of pregnancy. In the first trimester she may not be as ardent as she was before; it's not personal, so don't take it personally. If she is sick or just plain tired, delay making love to a time when she feels like it as much as you do.

As she enters the second trimester, her stomach will settle and her energy level will perk up some. Her sexual interest also perks up as she feels better and the baby is snuggled safely in the womb. All the goings-on in the uterus have stabilized, and you'll want each other more. There's usually no reason in this period not to have sex as often as you both like.

What will also change are the sexual positions possible for you as the baby grows. The missionary position (man above, woman below) will give way to woman above, man below, or you can enter her vagina from behind while lying on your side. By the middle trimester you will need to experiment to find the best way to satisfy you both and protect the baby as well.

Lovemaking is even more tricky in the final trimester, and especially in the last few weeks before delivery. Your partner's size is one factor, and your concern for your baby's welfare is another. If you are worried about premature labor, orgasm which causes the uterus to contract may be off limits, precluding masturbation or other stimulation as well. Hugging, kissing and snuggling may be your most viable alternatives for the time being.

Togetherness

Going through your partner's pregnancy hand-in-hand with her has two parts to it. One is the opportunity to build a profoundly important bond between you. The other is your discovery of emotional depths in yourself that you probably never guessed were there.

It doesn't happen by magic. It doesn't happen without confusion, mistakes, anger, disappointment and uncertainty—on both sides. But the testimony of fathers who have consciously chosen to come to terms with pregnancy leaves no doubt that the result can also lead to a stronger, more joyful relationship. And, in the future, it will include the baby who started it all.

2

Shouldering Your Share

Getting through pregnancy, planning a birth and setting up the practical mechanism of family living requires that both of you learn, think and plan with care. If you have done your planning well, and have taken on the responsibility for important decisions, you will feel more at ease later on when the baby is born and needs a father. It's a shoe that will fit, and you can start breaking it in early.

Meanwhile, back here at the beginning, let's start pulling apart the pieces that you and your partner must wrestle with. You will have to deal with surprises in a period that is neither serene nor consistent. So the more you know about what's ahead for you and your wife, the better you and she can plan and be prepared to confront contingencies with minimal fear and anxiety.

There are many important decisions to make for pregnancy, birth and baby care. To simplify that rather awesome task, here is an outline of the areas to focus on as you go along.

Each area in the list offers you opportunities to become actively involved in adapting your life to the new baby. When you and your partner form a consensus as to what you want and how you get it, there will be fewer surprises. You will be less likely to say, "I wish we could have . . ." or "Why did we . . . ?"

As you and your wife tackle each section, read up on the subject and talk to those who in your judgment have handled the situa-

DECISIONS, DECISIONS

1. What tasks around the house need doing and who should do them?

   ____ Laundry   ____ Vacuuming

   ____ Grocery shopping   ____ Clean kitchen

   ____ Cooking   ____ Clean bathroom(s)

   ____ Dishes   ____ Errands

   ____ Lawn-mowing and   ____ Special projects
         gardening

2. How involved do you want and expect to be in the birth of this baby?

   ____ Participate in selection of obstetrical medical team

   ____ Participate in selection of a suitable birth environment

   ____ Accompany wife on prenatal checkups

   ____ Participate in decision about prenatal testing

   ____ Attend childbirth education classes to prepare for coaching role

   ____ Practice labor breathing techniques with wife during pregnancy

3. How involved do you want and expect to be in nurturing your baby?

   ____ Shop for nursery furniture, car seat and baby clothes

   ____ Attend parenting preparation class for tips on taking care of the baby

   ____ Participate in the selection of the baby's doctor

   ____ Participate in making the decision between breast-feeding and bottle-feeding

4. What financial planning does your new family need?

   ____ Decide how you are going to pay for prenatal care, childbirth and postpartum care

   ____ Plan weekly or monthly budget for your family's income after the baby is born

tion well. Seek out several experts to get more than one or two opinions. To get you started, in this chapter we will discuss each of the areas in turn and try to help you do what is best for you and your family.

Help with the Housework

Start by thinking small, on a domestic scale. Even though you are exultant at this turn of events ("Wow! I'm going to be a father!"), down on the ground, where you live, the house still has to be cleaned, dishes washed, meals prepared, laundry done, food provided. As a philosopher once said, life is made up of one damned thing after another. They add up.

How you handle chores is a choice as individual as you and your partner. Paid help is one solution, great if you can afford it. If not, improvise your own plan that clearly states who does what. Assuming that your partner works, you're probably already sharing the chores and have a head start. Make a list of the chores, pare them down to the most essential ones, and take on as many yourself as you reasonably can. Some jobs can be delayed or reassigned.

TIP: Don't strive for a 50-50 balance. The fair balance, given the circumstances, may turn out to be 75-25, with your shoulders carrying the heavier load. Remember, your wife's body is undergoing changes during pregnancy and she won't be able to do the bending, stooping and lifting of heavy housework. (When she has to bend over, make sure she squats without bending her back.)

Being on the Front Line

Many men don't know if they want to be present during labor and childbirth, nor do they feel immediately confident about taking on the role of labor coach. It's an uncertain, intimidating experience. You may not feel ready. The task covers new, untried ground. There are so many questions you won't be able to answer beforehand:

- Will I vomit?
- Will I faint at the sight of blood?
- Can I face seeing the woman I love in pain and distress?
- As I've never done this before, will I just be in the way? Will I fail?

All these are legitimate questions. Though there are no certain ways to discover how you will handle childbirth before labor starts, there are ways to test your mettle: Watch the film on birth in a childbirth class and see how you react to the scenes. Think back to how you reacted in an emergency situation (any kind of emergency, not just a medical alert). Did you keep your wits about you? Your reactions in these circumstances will help you determine how you will weather childbirth.

You can further allay your fears by asking questions in prepared childbirth class (see page 24). Talk with other fathers in the class. You will discover that you are all sharing the same misgivings and self-doubts. You will soon learn that you are all sailing in the same boat.

If it is possible for you to be present at your baby's birth, it's worth a try. The worst that can happen is that you will have to leave. Later, if you feel better, you can return. But if you don't try, you'll never know (1) if you could have done it, (2) any part of your wife's experience, and (3) the first minutes of your baby's life.

Chances are that you will rise above yourself. Your weak stomach will be overruled by the importance of the moment. If the sight of the placenta or a certain medical procedure is distasteful, look away. By viewing childbirth films you can learn to anticipate what you don't want to see.

Just as you have been there from the beginning, you are also a key player during childbirth. Take part and be involved. You are needed to assist at your baby's birth. Your wife definitely cannot do it alone.

Your Birth Plan

A birth plan is the matrix of decisions that surrounds a labor and birth. What kind of atmosphere and medical trappings do you and your partner want for your birth experience? How much medical intervention do you want in the labor and birth process? Some procedures may be optional, like the intravenous needle; others, like the fetal monitor, are mandatory in hospitals. Other questions to consider in formulating a birth plan: When do we opt for pain medication? What can we do if a cesarean birth becomes a real possibility?

TIP: When formulating a birth plan or scenario for labor and delivery, keep in mind that there is no way to predict exactly what will happen or how your wife will react to it. You and your wife need to think about contingencies. Learn to phrase these sentences with "If . . ., then . . . ."

Hospital, Doctor, Nurse-Midwife

Hospitals vary widely in what they offer. You will have to do some homework to discover the facilities in your area that fit your needs and wants. Some offer family-centered birth experiences; some are sterile and impersonal. Others fall somewhere in the middle.

These days, hospitals are trying to get your business. Some woo pregnant couples with so-called Maternity Teas, where hospital policies and programs are explained and prizes given out. Gone are the old days of dry maternity tours. They want you. You can pick and choose.

Birth Centers

Alternative birth centers or ABCs, also called maternity centers, are stand-alone facilities which offer full prenatal, birth, newborn and postpartum services. They are designed for the medically low-risk woman (typically, a healthy woman in her 20s), and your wife would be in the care of a Certified Nurse-Midwife (see page 27), with staff obstetricians and pediatricians as backup. ABCs offer the professionalism of a hospital in an envi-

BIRTH PLAN CHECKLIST

_____ Husband can stay with wife throughout each step of preparation, labor and delivery

_____ What preparations are required before labor (enema, shave, intravenous needle, etc.)

_____ Flexibility of fetal monitor policy which enables woman in labor to walk or move around

_____ Availability of a certified nurse-midwife

_____ Availability of a birthing bed or birthing chair

_____ Labor and delivery can take place in the same room

_____ The couple in labor can participate in decisions about administering pain medication during labor

_____ The couple in labor will be advised as soon as possible of any potential problem, such as labor not progressing, fetal distress, etc.

_____ Hospital and doctor's policy on indications for a cesarean birth

_____ Hospital policy on husband's presence at a cesarean birth

_____ Hospital policy on the immediate hour after the baby is born

_____ Availability of rooming-in during recovery

ronment that encourages both partners to be actively involved in the birth of their baby.

As yet there are no uniform licensing criteria or standards set up for these centers. Each is different and may or may not meet quality-of-care and safety standards. ABCs are still few and far between. Most of them are located on the east and west coasts, usually in heavily populated areas, although they can be found scattered lightly across the country. For information, write or call The Cooperative Birth Center Network (3123 Gottschall Road, Perkiomenville, PA 18074; 215-234-8068).

Childbirth Education

One of the best places to get answers to many of your questions is your childbirth education class. These are classes you attend with your wife when she is in her seventh month of pregnancy. Once a week, the instructor will teach you and your partner breathing, relaxation and psychological techniques to cope with the pain of labor contractions. You will see a film of a birth and go step by step through the processes of labor, delivery and recovery.

Prepared childbirth methods travel under a variety of titles—Dick-Read's *Childbirth Without Fear* approach, the Lamaze method (the most popular in this country), Sheila Kitzinger's psychosexual theory and Dr. Robert Bradley's husband-coached childbirth are among the best known. There has also been some use of acupuncture and hypnotherapy, but they are not so much methods of natural childbirth as forms of natural anesthesia, because they do not rely on chemicals for their effects.

These methods fall into one of two categories. The psychoprophylactic school, with Lamaze at the head, seeks to deflect pain and teaches pain control through breathing, relaxation and distraction of the woman in labor. Lamaze philosophy requires a labor coach to support and encourage the laboring woman, focusing on each contraction as it comes.

The proponents of the latter school differ in emphasis but all rely on creating a positive psychological state to break the fear-tension-pain cycle so common in labor. The woman in labor learns to tune in to the baby and the physical process of birth as her body responds, using breathing and concentration techniques.

Your wife is in training just as an athlete is dedicated to conditioning his or her body. In class you will learn to simulate a contraction: A typical exercise is for you to pinch her—hard—on the knee or heel with increasing pressure while she practices using her breathing techniques to ignore the pain. We encourage you to practice daily as training will enable her to reduce, or even eliminate altogether, her need for pain-killing drugs. Get in the habit of breathing with her. Help her learn to relax her muscles and her thoughts. These sessions will get you in the habit of being her cheerleader and coach for the marathon ahead. You'll be ready!

TYPICAL MEDICAL PROCEDURES DURING LABOR AND CHILDBIRTH

Type	Function
Intravenous needle	Allows woman to receive glucose solution directly into her system, which keeps her from becoming dehydrated during labor, and to receive pain medication if indicated
Enema	Empties the bowel to eliminate pressure on the birth canal; often optional
Pubic shave	Hair around immediate area of episiotomy (see below) is shaved or clipped
Episiotomy	The incision(s) that enlarges the vaginal opening to accommodate the baby's head at birth and prevents tearing of tissues; may be optional
Fetal monitor	An external or internal monitor which records the frequency and length of the contractions and tracks the baby's heartbeat; it attaches externally with straps or belts around the woman's abdomen, or attaches internally via a tiny electrode to the baby's head; seldom optional

Professional Help

THE OBSTETRICIAN

One of the best sources of reassurance and support is the doctor or certified nurse-midwife you enlist for your prenatal care and childbirth. Your goal is to choose someone who can endorse your birth plan. Depending on the community where you live, this may not be possible. Your fall-back position is to find a doctor who has persuasive reasons for where he or she disagrees with you and is willing to discuss them with you both as adults, not as an all-wise teacher dealing with stubborn, ignorant children.

Try to avoid, of course, adopting a similar attitude toward the doctors you meet. You and your partner may be extremely well informed and feel confident in your opinions, but these are not the same as medical experience and professional judgment. It may be necessary to make compromises in order to assure your wife's safety and a successful delivery.

There's another reason for shopping around: the high and steadily rising cost of medical care. Only those with excellent medical insurance can ignore the doctor's fee in making a selection. This should be explicitly discussed at the outset.

THE CERTIFIED NURSE-MIDWIFE (CNM) ALTERNATIVE

Many couples these days are looking closely at professionals other than a doctor to provide routine prenatal care and attend their labor and delivery. The certified nurse-midwife is a viable alternative for low-risk pregnancies without medical complications. A CNM is a professional registered nurse who has completed an educational program on pregnancy, birth and the postpartum period and has passed national certification boards. CNMs are affiliated with a physician in private practice, a hospital or a health maintenance organization. They consult with physicians in the event of any medical problems, and will turn a case over to the physician if advisable.

A certified nurse-midwife sees pregnancy and childbirth as a natural experience. The great advantage of having a CNM on your team is that he or she will stay with your wife through each contraction and give you expert help while you coach her. CNMs also have expertise in being advocates for the laboring couple, whose preferences may not be top priority for busy, overworked hospital staff. If you would like information on who is available in your area, write or call the American College of Nurse-Midwives (1522 K Street, NW, Suite 1120, Washington, D.C. 20005; 202-289-0171).

Other Decisions: Tests During Pregnancy

SONOGRAMS

Ultrasound screening, like radar, bounces waves off the fetus and then translates the results into dots on a screen. This is a relatively new technology, and there is disagreement among professionals about the safety of the test for routine pregnancies. Little is known about long-term effects on the baby. Before allowing a test to be performed, be certain that there is a sound medical reason for administering it. If there is, the odds are good that the information it gives the doctor will outweigh the possible risks to the baby.

AMNIOCENTESIS AND CVS

Amniocentesis is recommended for women over 35 to flag fetuses with chromosomal abnormalities such as Down's syndrome. A woman must wait 15 to 19 weeks after conception to have the test done. A needle is inserted carefully (using a sonogram to guide the technician) into the amniotic sac that cushions the baby while in the uterus. A small amount of amniotic fluid is withdrawn and cultured in a lab for two to six weeks. The technique has been perfected over the years, but still carries a low risk of miscarriage.

A new chromosomal test, Chorionic Villus Sampling, or CVS, has come into use recently and several institutions currently perform it. The catheter involved in the sampling has been governmentally approved but it is sold only to physicians who have been trained in its use. As their number increases, the test may well replace amniocentesis.

CVS can be done as early as the eighth week after conception.

Using a sonogram as a guide, the technician inserts a flexible plastic catheter through the vagina into the cervix. A small piece of the chorion (the early placenta which supports the baby with nutrients and oxygen) is removed. Because chorion cells are actively growing when removed and require no culturing, test results are ready in about a week.

Women experience no pain and the test can be completed in 15 minutes or so. So far the only women who are advised not to have the test are those who are susceptible to miscarriage or who have experienced bleeding during their pregnancy.

NOTE: Positive results from either test require the couple to make an intensely personal decision about whether the pregnancy should be allowed to continue.

Choosing a Doctor for Your Baby

Your medical adviser is a good source of names. Ask friends you trust, too. Sometimes one or two names will keep reappearing. This is both good and bad: The doctor is probably overworked and too busy for the extra attention you may feel you want, but he or she may also offer the best care in town.

CHECKPOINTS TO CONSIDER

Choose a pediatrician who:

- is conveniently located.
- is affiliated with the hospital you prefer.
- has convenient calling hours (for those small, but important questions that all new parents ask).
- has partners or backup doctors whom you trust.
- if your wife plans to nurse your baby, supports breast-feeding wholeheartedly (not all pediatricians do).
- is up-to-date on the latest pediatric trends and findings.
- will be on hand in the hospital to examine the baby within 24 hours after birth.

In metropolitan areas, it is an accepted practice to interview pediatricians before the baby is born. Personal interviews will help assure you that you are making the best choice. Comparing your notes and impressions, you and your wife can settle on someone who fits your needs. In smaller communities, word of mouth and referrals are your only resources.

Baby Accessories

Before the baby comes, you will need to buy or borrow a crib and, if you have a car, a car safety seat.

A crib should be sturdy and stable, have short corner posts (knobs are hazardous), and have adjustable mattress levels, so that you can lower the mattress as the baby grows. If you are considering a secondhand crib, whether purchased or borrowed, make sure that none of the pieces is missing and that the crib slats are no more than 2⅜ inches apart so that your baby's head cannot get caught in between them.

Whether you are buying an infant seat, a convertible seat (which can be adjusted for an infant or a toddler), or a toddler safety seat, it should meet the requirements of Federal Motor Vehicle Safety Standard 213, be easy to use, and must fit in your car without obstructing your rear view. It is extremely important to install the seat properly; if it is improperly installed, the seat will be less safe for your baby.

IMPORTANT SAFETY TIP: Make a habit of using the safety seat every time you drive anywhere with the baby. A seat that isn't used won't protect your baby.

Financial Planning

There are many additional expenses to squeeze into your budget during these months before your baby comes. Unless you have someone to give you what you need for your baby, you will have to invest in other nursery furniture as well as the crib, something to carry the baby in (a cloth carrier, stroller or carriage) as well as a safety seat for traveling in the car—and, of course, baby clothes and other necessities.

Your wife will have additional expenses to safeguard her health and the baby's during her pregnancy and after the baby is born. She will need vitamin supplements while she is pregnant and if she breast-feeds.

She will need more frequent dental checkups, too. Because of hormonal changes in a pregnant woman's body, her gums can become exceedingly sensitive and develop an unhealthy appearance, bleeding readily during brushing or flossing. Professional cleaning every three months or even once a month during pregnancy may be necessary to control the condition. Plan for the cost. Health insurance plans that include dental care are still uncommon.

Insurance, Or It's More Fun to Read the Phone Book

Unless you habitually read the documents that control your destiny, such as the lease on your apartment, the terms of your home mortgage and your credit card contract, you probably don't know the extent of your medical insurance coverage. Though reading insurance documents is slow going, it is also very important. As soon as possible, set aside time to scrutinize your policy.

Look for what it *doesn't* include. Deductibles are steadily rising, "comprehensive" may not mean what it says, and obstetric (and related maternity costs) and well-baby care are *not* covered in many policies. Read the small print, the footnotes, the provisos. Every word in an insurance policy counts. Don't confuse hospital coverage with medical/surgical coverage.

To penetrate the professional jargon on your own may seem like a forbidding task, and you may be tempted to take a lot for granted. Press on. Ask around. It's not unlikely that a friend has already broken the code and can either interpret your policy for you, or at least help you with the language.

Many books and publications also translate the special terminology of insurance policies into understandable language. And

---

WHEN TWO INCOMES BECOME ONE

Couples enjoying two salaries feel a pinch when the wife drops out of the workaday world after the baby is born. If it's doubtful that two can live as cheaply as one, it's even more unlikely that three can.

What to do? Try taking a financial dry run during pregnancy. Design a budget, using only the income you plan to live on. See how it goes for a month or two. As you try it out, two things will happen:

1. You will be able to iron out the problems, and
2. You will be saving money by banking the second salary.

---

you have a perfect right to go to your carrier's representative and request information.

If your wife is covered by your policy at work and her own employee coverage as well, watch out for dual coverage. The overlap can sometimes result in waivers or restrictive conditions.

HMO: An Insurance Alternative

A health maintenance organization (HMO) is a community of doctors and other medical specialists, often including laboratory and radiology services. They provide continuous medical care to their members, with all the auxiliary services needed along the way, for a fixed, prepaid monthly fee. They dissolve the traditional equation that kept medical insurers on one side and the professionals who deliver the health care on the other. Both are in the same shop.

Having joined an HMO, you, your partner and the baby after arrival receive virtually unlimited medical care for the monthly fee. This is pay-as-you-go care available under conventional health insurance policies.

Sounds too good to be true, you figure, and there has to be a catch, like huge fees for such a comprehensive service without the exclusions, limitations, deductions and "reasonable and customary" fee restrictions typical in standard policies?

Not so. A number of studies have shown that HMO premiums are lower than those of traditional insurers while, most important, benefits are much broader. Increasing costs continue to boost fees in both camps, but the evidence suggests that HMO premiums are rising about half as fast as those of old-line health insurance companies.

But the money you save at an HMO may not be worth it, because it may not offer the important emotional support and confidence that a one-on-one relationship with a private practitioner often provides. HMOs operate under a kind of anonymity, or impersonality. HMOs are communal institutions and doctors are, in a very real sense, interchangeable. Thus your wife may not have the opportunity to develop the trusting, supportive relationship with a doctor that is so stabilizing during the often anxious, uncertain months of pregnancy. You and she may prize the relationship with her medical adviser, and feel there's no substitute for his or her intimate knowledge of the pregnancy.

With an HMO you can't choose which doctor you have. There's no guarantee, for example, that your wife will always see the same obstetrician during her pregnancy; moreover, childbirth will be attended by the obstetrician who is on duty at the hospital. So, you and your wife may not be familiar with this doctor at a very sensitive and vulnerable moment in your lives. (A non-HMO team of obstetricians also rotates duty on nights and weekends, so if your baby is born outside regular business hours, you may not get your own doctor in that case either.)

Because of the payment system, HMO doctors are inclined to be sensitive to costs and can be cautious in calling for treatment that may skew the unit's budget. HMOs, even those that are non-profit, are not philanthropies; they have to control expenses. This can mean that a decision may not be made until the doctors agree that a proposed treatment is, in fact, both the most economical and the most effective.

Ready and Eager

In this chapter we have approached pregnancy as a period of decisions for both you and your wife. As it draws to a close, you will feel better prepared—on paper, at least—for labor and child-birth. Working together on all these crucial matters will make you both eager for the future to arrive.

"Together"—that's the magic word.

3

Labor and Birth

During the last months of pregnancy your role as ally and friend to your wife is particularly important. By acting as coach-advocate during pregnancy and childbirth and, later after the baby is born, nurturing the baby as well as providing for him, you will become a family man in the truest sense.

If you roll up your sleeves and plunge into the fathering experience, you will be repaid a thousand times. It's value added all the way, both for you and for your wife. By working with her to manage the pain of childbirth and by witnessing the birth of your baby, you'll be on the inside of an event so momentous that it defies description.

Fathers, in the attempt to attach words to it, try "awe," "amazement," "reborn" (themselves), "overcome," and report feeling a rush of love for their wives that exceeded any emotion they had ever experienced.

When you reach the end of this chapter you will be holding your baby—at least in your imagination. An amazing thought indeed. But before you and your wife get to that moment, there's the task of labor and childbirth to get through. It is our intent to show you that it isn't as overwhelming as it may at first seem. Like any big project, you start at the beginning, take it step by step, and before you know it, it's done.

Whose Baby Is It Anyway?

You and your wife should approach childbirth with completely open minds. There will be an abundance of opinions offered, but remember—every birth experience is different, and is an event that, in the truest sense, belongs to the parents alone.

Indeed, you can do much to strengthen that critical sense of ownership by thinking in terms of "giving birth." "Delivery" is a term that pushes the parents, chiefly the mother-to-be, off center stage and suggests that the medical team are the principal players. But the fact is that, however indispensable they may be in complicated or emergency situations, they are outsiders in this main event of your life, and you will not depreciate their contribution by regarding them as such. You and your wife have the power to retain control of this landmark moment in your life together.

LABOR AND CHILDBIRTH: AN OVERVIEW

You'll be better able to support your wife through labor to the birth of your baby if you know the phases of childbirth and how each affects her. Here's a quick overview plus some practical suggestions about how you can help.

"Labor" is a well-chosen word assigned to the efforts a woman's body makes to force the baby out of the uterus (womb) into the world. A series of contractions, not unlike the regular flexing of biceps, increases in frequency, duration and intensity until the baby is born. This is called labor because it is hard work—very hard work. In fact, it is a marathon of truly Olympian proportions.

As we have said, there is no way to predict what your wife's first labor will be like. In subsequent pregnancies her first experience may be a general guide to what will occur—but surprises may happen. Like the proverbial Boy Scout: Be prepared.

The Stages of Childbirth

THE FIRST STAGE

The work of the first stage is the flattening or effacement and the opening up of the cervix (the mouth of the uterus) to ten centimeters, also described as "five fingers." This is the longest stage, lasting on average from 12 to 18 hours.

As the cervix dilates, your wife must cope with increasingly intense assaults of pain. As her labor coach, you must help her to combat the fear and tension that severe pain creates. Tenderness and encouragement will help her to relax and to brave the next contraction and the one after that.

THE ONSET OF LABOR

Because the early contractions are mild, usually no more intense than premenstrual cramps, it isn't always clear that true labor has started. Indeed, women sometimes experience false labor which has contractions that are similar to those of "true" labor. The difference lies in their irregularity and the fact that they go away when the woman moves around. If the membranes of the amniotic sac rupture, also called "the waters breaking," there is no doubt that labor has begun. *But remember: True labor can begin with the amniotic sac intact.* Once the bag of water breaks, contractions may increase in intensity and efficiency.

When the clear amniotic fluid gushes out, it happens without warning (unless your birth attendant decides to puncture the bag artificially—a speedy and completely painless procedure). Because the fluid comes through the vaginal opening, there is no way to hold it back until a toilet is handy. The only way to prepare for it is for your wife to line your bed with a waterproof sheet and keep a thick bath towel handy wherever she goes (in the family car, a shopping bag, or the grocery cart, etc.).

The first stage can be divided into three parts, each of which is successively shorter in duration:

Conversational Phase: The cervix dilates from one to four centimeters. As the name implies, this is the least intense phase, with contractions coming six to 15 minutes apart. You should alert your medical team and follow their instructions about when to go to the hospital.

Active Phase: The cervix dilates from four to seven centimeters. Pain is more intense now, with contractions coming every three to five minutes.

Transition: The cervix dilates from seven to ten centimeters. Pain is at its peak, with contractions coming every 90 seconds. There may only be a rest of 30 seconds between the end of one contraction and the onset of the next.

TIP: If your watch has a stop-watch function or a second hand, use it to help her time the contractions. When you are timing contractions, mark the intervals from the beginning of one to the beginning of the next one.

THE SECOND STAGE

Your wife enters this stage when she has dilated the full ten centimeters and is encouraged by the medical team to push. The baby descends into the birth canal and is born. The baby moves out of the uterus, turns to face nose down (facing your partner's spine) and inches past the tailbone and pubic bone. If the baby's head turns properly, this stage is usually not particularly painful. If the baby has difficulties maneuvering through the passage, this stage can be quite prolonged.

If your wife has been in a traditional labor room, she will be moved to the delivery room. Once she is on the delivery table, either you or a labor nurse will need to help her elevate her upper torso so she can get a good angle for bearing down during contractions. As before, she will rest between contractions.

BACK LABOR

If the baby is facing away from your wife's spine and is "sunny side up," the head presses on her tailbone, causing severe back labor pain.

The good news is that you can relieve much of her discomfort by applying strong, constant counterpressure to her lower back and buttocks. Pressing tennis balls or a wallpaper roller against her (she'll direct you where) saves your arms from giving out.

THE THIRD STAGE

Your wife pushes out the placenta or afterbirth. Until now the placenta has been the life support system that brings fresh blood containing nutrients and oxygen to the baby and removes the waste from the baby's circulation. Now it is no longer needed and it disengages from the uterus. This process usually lasts only a short time, with a few mild contractions needed to push it out. To encourage its expulsion, a labor nurse may massage or push on her abdomen. Keep in mind that during this phase, your baby has already been born. Your mind—as well as your wife's—is occupied with your new baby. This stage occurs without much conscious effort or attention.

The Power of Two

The word "coach" has its origins on the athletic playing fields of America. The image is clear: She is the athlete with a marathon to win; you are the trainer, dedicated to her success. As an athlete must train for an event, she must practice endlessly. She must condition her muscles and condition her behavior. You, as her trainer, are actively involved in making sure that she is ready.

Then, when the time comes, you are committed to her throughout the ordeal. You must concentrate with her through every contraction. But there is a good deal more to it than the mental energy involved. You can really help her.

Don't underestimate the power of massage and counterpressure for back labor. Any other comfort measures you can offer will make a big difference to her morale. Don't expect much in the way of "please" and "thank you." She probably won't be able to do much more than grunt or moan her appreciation.

As labor progresses, she will be less able to ask for what she needs or wants. When that happens, you will be in the position of having to take an educated guess as to what to do for her. By that time you will have already logged in several hours and you'll probably know what works and what she wants.

Finally, let's say a word about how *you* are going to get through all those hours in labor. When you are on the outside looking in, it may be hard to imagine taking on a job that is so intense and that takes such a long time to finish. But when she's laboring with concentration, time, in effect, stands still. If you are concentrating with her and are actively involved in alleviating her pain, you too will be only vaguely aware of the clock.

A LABOR COACH KIT TO BRING TO THE HOSPITAL

- This book
- Newspapers, magazines and a favorite book to read aloud if labor is slow
- A radio or tape player with favorite tapes
- Quick energy snacks for you
- A razor, toothbrush, and clean shirt
- Address book and change for pay phone
- A camera loaded with film

For her comfort:

- A favorite pillow
- Lip balm, talcum powder, body lotion
- Tennis balls or a wallpaper roller for counterpressure
- Lollipops

HOW A LABOR COACH CAN HELP

Here are some specifics that you can do to get her through the long hours of labor. Keep this list with you in labor as a reminder.

- Massage her back muscles till your own arms ache.
- Offer her ice chips.
- Breathe or chant with her.
- Read to her or talk idly to pass the time.
- Rally her morale with a pep talk.
- Time her contractions so she knows how far she has to go before she can rest again.
- Adjust the pillows or birthing bed.
- Help her change positions.
- Walk her around to speed up a sluggish labor.
- Press tennis balls or a wallpaper roller against her back and buttocks to provide counterpressure against back labor.
- In the last stage of dilation, help her resist the urge to push.
- Elevate her upper torso when she must push the baby and the afterbirth out.

Waiting for the Stork

There is nothing magical about a due date. Even if it was cal-culated accurately, using the correct date for the beginning of the last period, and your wife's menstrual cycle is regular, the baby still may come at any time two weeks before or after the actual day. So you will be kept guessing—which is excellent training for parenting later on!

As the countdown begins, you will stick close to the phone. You'll be reluctant to take a long lunch hour and anxious if you become stuck somewhere in traffic. If the due date comes and goes, your nerves will start to fray. If she has false labor (contrac-tions that are erratic and disappear if she moves around), tem-pers may become even thinner. Try not to be so anxious. Remem-ber: Once your baby comes, he'll stay.

If there is reason to believe that your wife's pregnancy has been

CATCH 22: CESAREAN BIRTH

A cesarean birth is abdominal surgery that is performed in a regular operating room for various reasons: Fetal distress (stress to the baby caused by a lack of oxygen during labor), lack of progress during labor, and a previous cesarean birth are common causes. (These days, more and more doctors are willing, in certain circumstances, to allow a woman to labor and experience vaginal childbirth despite a previous cesarean birth.) Anatomical reasons are often cited as well: The baby may be too big or the mother's pelvis may be too small.

If there is a physical reason that is determined before labor begins (you may want to have another doctor give a second opinion on the subject), your wife will be able to make an appointment for surgery. If your wife has epidural anesthesia (a local), she will be awake during delivery, and, depending on hospital policy, you may be permitted into the operating room.

Many cesareans are performed after labor has begun and there isn't always time for a local anesthetic to be administered. In cases such as these, a general anesthetic is used and fathers are not usually allowed into the operating room.

This fact underscores the importance of contingency planning. One decision can lead to another in a chain of events. Consider carefully the course you take. But even careful planning cannot ensure that the road during childbirth won't take an unexpected turn. Even the best laid plans can backfire.

One birth in five is cesarean. If your childbirth education class has ten couples in it, two are likely to have a cesarean birth. You look around the room at all these pregnant women and think, "It won't be us." But you never know. It's as likely to be you as anyone else.

Note: If your wife does have a cesarean, and especially if she has a general anesthetic, be prepared for her to have a slower and more uncomfortable recovery period after the baby is born. Your support and understanding will go a long way to help.

prolonged past 42 weeks or that the placenta is not functioning properly, your medical team will probably induce her labor. Her amniotic sac may be broken first, and then she may be given the drug oxytocin in an intravenous needle. Another catalyst for labor is the synthetic hormone prostaglandin, administered as a suppository, gel or tablet.

TIP: If her labor does not start spontaneously, and the medical team induces labor, she will skip the easy-going early phase of labor and have intense contractions right from the start.

Ready, Set, Go!

CONVERSATIONAL PHASE

If labor starts in the evening or the middle of the night, you should both try to rest. You have a long haul ahead and both of you will be better for facing it refreshed. Early labor is not particularly uncomfortable. It is more likely that excitement rather than pain will prevent sleep. Once you're sure that true labor has started, your wife's diet must be restricted to a little clear liquid like broth or sugar tea. You should follow the recommendation of your medical team. You, of course, can chow down, if you feel like it—but do it discreetly!

Follow your medical adviser's instructions as to when to alert your medical team. Most physicians and certified nurse-midwives want to know when the contractions are steadily coming about ten to 12 minutes apart, or when her water breaks, with or without contractions. Any unusual or painful discomforts should be reported as well.

ACTIVE PHASE

As labor progresses and contractions intensify, she loses her ability to carry on a conversation and communicates her needs with grunts and moans. You must help her to relax, conserve her energy and stay confident. As the going gets rougher, all three become increasingly difficult.

Here is when the routine practice of the past weeks pays off. Anxiety and tension are the enemies, for they act to undermine her control of the situation. "You can do it, you can do it," is an effective chant for some coaches. Your demonstration of total confidence in her, of your support and attention, are the greatest contributions you can make.

A few words of caution. In the beginning of labor (when the cervix dilates to four centimeters), the spirits of expectant parents run high. There is excitement because the long-awaited event is finally at hand, and discomfort is minimal.

As labor intensifies, the fun stops and serious business begins. Anticipation fades. An invisible wall goes up around the laboring woman. She seems remote and will show little recognition or appreciation of the efforts you're making on her behalf. She can't. The contractions, coming more quickly and intensely now, absorb all her energy. She hears you. She knows what you're doing, but she can't make the effort to tell you so. All her resources are concentrated on her contractions and resting in between them.

TRANSITION

This is the crescendo and usually mercifully short, lasting an hour or two. Contractions are coming fast and are at the height

---

IMAGERY RELAXATION

Some experts advise a relaxation technique that has its origins in Eastern meditation practices. Called "imagery relaxation," it entails your verbally painting pictures of particularly tranquil scenes. These could be real places you and your partner have enjoyed together, or inventions. You could dream up a peaceful river down which you and she float in a canoe, with the sun dancing on the water. Or you could remind her of a favorite beach and tell her that you are rubbing her with suntan lotion! Add details as they come to you.

---

of intensity. She has almost no time to rest. Indeed, she may doze during the 30 to 45 seconds of rest time between, and wake to another 60 to 90 seconds of contraction. The fact that she dozes between contractions helps to sustain her during this difficult phase, but it is also hard on her because whenever she is awake, she is having a contraction.

Women react variously to the pain of this process. A few remain quiet, but many become angry, impatient and short-tempered. It is important to remember not to take it personally. Now's the time for encouraging words, even if she is swearing a blue streak. It's a great sign! Alert the staff to be ready because you're almost there.

PUSHING

When the nurse-midwife or physician determines that she is fully dilated, she will get the go-ahead to push. This is a relief for many women. She can give in to the urge to push, and the pressure she exerts when bearing down is likely to erase the pain felt during earlier contractions. (As we mentioned earlier, however, if the baby doesn't rotate, she will be in as much pain, if not more pain, than she was in transition.) She is no longer passively getting through, she is actively engaged. Pushing is hard work. It may last a half hour or several hours. Give her frequent progress reports as the head appears and then disappears between contractions (your partner's eyes close with the effort of pushing; she won't see it).

TIP: As she enters the second stage there will be moments when she can't bear down when she has the urge to do so: When she is being transferred to the delivery table and when the episiotomy incision is being performed are two points when she *must* resist her impulse to push. If she has been practicing controlling these muscles by doing her childbirth exercises, these efforts will pay off now. Help her stay in control by encouraging her to relax and breathing with her during these crucial periods.

Here at Last!

And then that moment comes that you and your partner have worked over for many months. The baby's head crowns, your baby's hair is visible. The vision you see is hypnotizing. Wake up! If you have brought a camera along, have it at the ready to take pictures.

Soon the head clears the vaginal opening and the shoulders follow. A moment later the baby slips out. Shortly afterward, you are holding a new creature in your arms. Your baby! He is truly beautiful. It doesn't matter that he is blue, wrinkled and still covered with packing material. It doesn't matter that he looks like Jonathan Winters. He has changed your life forever. Things come and go, but you will always be this child's daddy. You have entered into fatherhood, stage one.

4

Real Men Are Daddies

Amazingly, after the ordeal of birth, the baby is quietly alert, ready to start puzzling out the new world she has fallen into. She will remain so for about an hour before she drifts off to sleep. This first hour can be a special time for you and your wife to get to know your baby.

If there have been no special complications in childbirth, the two of you will be left for awhile with your baby before she is taken off to the nursery. Take turns holding the baby. Your wife may be feeling shaky and need you to support her arm while she holds the baby. If she is going to breast-feed, she may want to put the baby to her breast.

If your wife has had a cesarean birth or if circumstances don't permit the initial hour together, don't worry. Whenever it is that you begin holding and nurturing your baby, you will still cover the same ground. Hours, days and weeks lie ahead full of opportunities for you to get to know one another.

A New You

When your baby is born and you finally leave the room where it happened, you will certainly feel tired and relieved. And you may also discover a tangible difference in the way you see yourself

WHAT HAPPENS IMMEDIATELY AFTER BIRTH

Mother	Baby
Nurse massages uterus externally	Cord clamped and cut
Local anesthetic is admin-	Nose and throat suctioned
istered and episiotomy sewn	Weighed, cleaned and
up (with stitches that will	footprinted
gradually dissolve)	Eye drops, Vitamin K shot
Sucks on lollipop or ice chips	given
and rests	Physical Apgar test
May breast-feed and hold baby	

and the rest of the world. You may feel stronger and more capable than ever before.

You may be so excited and proud of your baby that you can't wait to show her off. Seeing, holding and touching her are bound to be exhilarating experiences. In fact, you may feel that this is the greatest baby in the whole history of the world!

If you have been able to enjoy your baby during the first hour after birth, you may decide to go home for some well-deserved rest. Or your system may still be charged with excitement and you may want to remain. Your baby will usually be transferred to the nursery and your wife will be moved either to a recovery room or her own hospital bed. You may find yourself shuttling back and forth with up-to-the-minute status reports. If your wife is as supercharged with excitement as you are, you will probably want to share the experience with the only other person in the world who can appreciate it.

Don't worry if you aren't so ecstatic. Circumstances and personality determine how a man reacts to the drama of birth. Becoming a father is subject to all the variables and uncertainties inherent in human nature. It is hard to predict exactly how you will feel. Don't anticipate or force how you feel. Be patient. Give yourself time to experience your baby. You'll enjoy it more if you don't attach pre-established expectations to the enjoyment.

WHAT'S THE SCORE?

Almost immediately after your baby is born, the attending pediatrician or pediatric nurse will screen the baby to determine if she is healthy and breathing properly and what special care, if any, may be needed in the nursery. The test most commonly used is the Apgar, taken one minute after birth and again five minutes after birth. It rates your baby's physical adjustment to independent living on a scale from zero to ten points. A one-minute rating below *five* may not mean much; a five-minute Apgar score below *five* is possibly significant. There's no need for concern if your baby's score is off one or two points. That's fairly common.

Here's how the Apgar table looks:

	0	1	2
Heart rate	Absent	Under 100 per minute	Over 100 per minute
Respiratory effort	Absent	Slow, gasping	Good, strong cry
Muscle tone	Flaccid	Poor	Active motion
Reflexes	No response	Grimace, some response	Active, crying
Color	Body pale or blue	Body pink, extremities blue	Completely pink

Hospital Miscellany

ROOMING-IN

If the hospital allows rooming-in, i.e., allows your baby to be in the hospital room with you and your wife for all or part of the day, and if your wife feels up to it, it is a great way to get to know your new baby. You will get used to holding her, diapering her, feeding her with a bottle of water. If your wife is nursing, she will have more opportunities to feed the baby.

SIBLING VISITS

Some hospitals allow an older child to visit the hospital. It is often helpful for him or her to see the new baby (through the nursery window) and understand that Mom is okay. If your facility does not allow such visits, make sure your wife calls home every day. In the latter case, you may be obliged to stay at home more so that you can be with your older child.

CIRCUMCISION

If you have a boy baby, you and your wife will have to decide if you want him circumcised, a procedure which removes the foreskin that covers the tip of the penis. As there is no evidence that the foreskin, if left intact, is a potential breeding ground for infection, the decision is a personal one for parents, and will be influenced by cultural or religious concerns rather than by hygiene.

JAUNDICE

If, a couple of days after your baby is born, her skin takes on a color reminiscent of a Florida tan, she has a common condition called jaundice. It is due to an inability of her liver to handle excess red blood cells, which are broken down into a substance called bilirubin. The condition usually disappears within a week.

The hospital will monitor the "bili count" by checking your baby's blood with a heel-prick blood test or a hand-held jaundice meter that measures light reflected from the baby's skin. If the bili count becomes too high (although the policy varies from hospital to hospital, 6 to 7 milligrams/100 milliliters serum found in blood is considered safe, 10 to 12 is usually acceptable, and over 15 is unsafe), they will probably put her under special lights for a day or two.

Becoming a Family

BONDING

When you hold your baby, you see a real live human being, wide-eyed and quiet, looking back at you. The contact between you is real. Hold on to these precious moments, because this time can be the entrance into a whole new dimension of your life as a man.

Now that the baby is bundled and nestled in your arms, you will be aware of a tremendous sense of fulfillment. This is only the first step in your growth as a nurturer and provider for this tiny, helpless being. The fathering "instinct," like the maternal "instinct," must be learned. To be successfully integrated into fathering, you must discover who your baby is. You must "bond" with her.

The word is misleading, though. Bonding suggests an action that happens once and is immediately accomplished, as in carpentry or welding; it has mechanical overtones. As we all know, you build human relationships over time; they don't just happen automatically. We suggest that you think, instead, of "attachment," which better expresses the evolution of the connection between father and child.

The key here is physical closeness. There are lots of ways to accomplish this. Hold her every chance you get. Once you are home, carry her in a cloth carrier on your chest on a walk or while you do errands. You will feel her warmth and movements. Body to body, you will begin to communicate: You will feel her dependence; she will feel your protection. As you log time with your baby, you will notice that your feeling for her intensifies.

The bonding process will accelerate if you expand your duties to include taking care of her day-to-day needs. Share the nurturing load (though, naturally, you must work within certain biological and personal limitations).

COMING HOME

The early euphoria of fatherhood will get a boost when you bring your wife and baby home. You've looked forward with such eagerness to this moment. Coming home alone to a dark, blank house after visiting hours are over hasn't been much fun.

If you drove your wife *to* the hospital in a controlled hysteria, you may find that you drive her and the baby home *from* the hospital as if you were carrying a load of eggs. (Remember to install the car safety seat before you go to pick them up. Some hospitals won't release the baby unless you have one.) When you arrive home with your precious cargo, you will be happy that the three of you are finally together under your own roof, not in a hospital room, where you were always a visitor.

Once they have left the professional baby support system provided by the hospital, fathers and mothers alike can feel apprehension and doubt their ability and resources to do the job. A newborn baby's sleep and eating patterns are disorganized; she cries a lot. Parents are not sure what the baby needs, or when she needs it. It will be two to six weeks before their baby settles down to a predictable schedule.

CRYING TIMES

It is important to remember, as you and your wife work through these early weeks, that your baby has no more idea of what's going on than you do. You won't always be able to fix the problem. In the early going, parenting is based on the not-so-scientific method of trial and error. A baby cries for reasons other than hunger and fatigue, and she won't be able to sit up and tell you. You will develop a repertoire of techniques for these cranky times which will often soothe the baby and help her to stop crying.

Babies often cry during the cocktail/dinner hour. For no apparent reason your baby is inconsolable. You can be a big help. You can take over dinner while your wife nurses and calms her. Alternatively, you may find yourself at the helm of the baby carriage, making consecutive circles around the block. Going for a ride in the car can work wonders, too.

Other solutions for other crying times: You may find that placing her on her tummy over your knees and gently patting or rubbing her back will help to bring up a gas bubble. Or she may be crying because she is bored being in one position. Try turning her from her back to her tummy, or vice versa.

DEVELOPING A MENTAL CHECKLIST

The only way your baby can tell you something is wrong is by crying. You will learn to respond to her cue by running down a list of possible causes. You will start with the most likely one and move down the list until an answer is found—or at least she has stopped crying.

- Is she hungry?
- Is she tired?
- Is she bored?
- Is she overstimulated?
- Is she ill (feverish, drawing up her legs in pain or showing other signs of discomfort)?
- Is she upset because the people around her are upset? (Babies pick up on the moods of others from a very early age.)
- Is she feeling lonely and needs some cuddling? (Don't worry that picking her up will "spoil" her—you can't spoil a young baby.)

Experiment with motion. She will usually quieten when you pick her up, put her over your shoulder and walk around. A ride in a cloth carrier on Daddy's chest will often soothe the unhappiest baby.

THIS IS NOT A CONTEST

Go with whatever works, but be ready to improvise when you discover that what works one day won't work the next. *Don't* take it personally if she doesn't stop. *Don't* see it as success or failure. Too often new parents equate their ability to soothe their baby with their ability to nurture their baby. *Don't* put your ego on the line.

This is not a contest with your partner to see who can dry tears faster. Of course, you want the baby to be comfortable and happy. All parents want the best for their baby. The problem is—now and later—that it can't always be. Babies are hardy creatures. They survived the rather harrowing birth experience. They can

THE FOOTBALL HOLD

Many a father enjoys carrying his baby around like a football. This leaves one arm free for other duties. You can try it, too:

SUNNY SIDE UP: In the first weeks after birth, when the baby can't hold her head up at all, lay her on her back, cradling her head in your hand. Align her body along your arm. Her legs will naturally fold up into the fetal position. Rest your arm on your body for added support of her body.

THE FLIP SIDE: As she learns to hold her head off the mattress when lying on her tummy, she will have sufficient strength to hold her head up while she lies on her tummy along your arm. Hold her shoulders and upper chest in your hand and allow her legs to straddle the crook of your elbow. As with the earlier hold, rest your arm on your body to help support her body.

survive inexperienced parenting with ease. Your baby will thrive both because of you and in spite of you.

Differences Unite

Daddies deal with their babies quite differently from mommies. They handle them in a much more physical way. Mommies are gentle and careful, and worry over details of the baby's comfort. You greet her, play with her, hold and carry her in ways that are all your own. Don't let the differences you see bother you. They are both natural and desirable.

Your baby probably wouldn't have it any other way. If it were possible to have two people acting in exactly the same way, how boring it would be! You can be sure that she is taking everything in; infants are knowledge sponges. She will respond to each of you differently. She is learning that there's value in differences. Can you imagine anything more important for her than discovering that there's spontaneity in life, surprise and love that aren't defined by an off-the-shelf formula?

A word or two of caution, however. In the early weeks after birth, a newborn must assimilate a lot of new sensations. Leaving the dark security of the womb, she enters our bright, airy world jammed with stimulation. She discovers hunger, texture and space for the first time. Overstimulation can prolong her period of adjustment. Later, as she learns to sit, crawl and walk, she is rapidly expanding the world she knows by leaps and bounds. She may find spontaneity too much to handle at the end of the day or when she is ready for a nap. Don't overdo a good thing.

Feeding Your Baby

The decision between bottle- and breast-feeding is very personal and it is best if you participate in the selection. You and your wife will have to weigh many important variables in making the choice. Your baby's nutrition, your wife's career or job, and your attitudes and expectations are some factors to consider. Get the facts about both methods. Examine your feelings and weigh the pros and cons.

BREAST-FEEDING

If your wife nurses your baby, you will not be able to feed the baby on a regular basis. The only bottles she will get will be occasional relief bottles. But there is satisfaction in the knowledge that your baby is getting nature's perfect food along with some important immunities against certain diseases. You can find alternate ways to care for your baby. If she enjoys a bath, you can take over that routine as a way to soothe her and be close to her.

As your wife and baby settle into breast-feeding, they become a nursing couple. Their closeness may seem to shut you out. This feeling of alienation can hurt and fester unless you talk it over with your wife. Communicating your feelings will help defuse the problem.

BATHTIME STRATEGIES

It's not nearly as difficult as you probably think it is to give your baby a bath:

NEWBORNS should have a sponge bath *without soap.* All you need is a soft washcloth, a small container of warm (but not hot) water, some cotton balls, a mild baby shampoo, a contoured baby bath sponge for her to lie on, a soft towel, cream if needed, a fresh diaper and a change of clothes. Make sure the room is warm enough and that you have everything before you start. Handle her firmly, but gently. *Never* leave her unattended, even for a moment.

1. Gently undress the baby except for her diaper in the same place where you are going to bathe her. Lay her on the sponge.

2. Rinse the cloth in water and wring it out. Rinse again as needed to keep the cloth warm.

3. Gently wipe her arms, legs and body with the cloth, stopping to dry her as you go. To wash her back, raise her off the sponge, supporting her head with one hand, and wipe with the other.

4. Next, remove the diaper. Clean up any mess with tissues. Then with your wet washcloth wipe the genital and anal areas, paying special attention to the folds and creases. Wipe her bottom from front to back. Gently dry her, smooth on cream and put on a fresh diaper.

5. Wet and squeeze out the cotton balls and wipe her face and ears. Don't poke into her nose. If you spy some dry mucus, you can roll an end of a damp cotton ball into a small point and dab gently up to loosen and remove it.

6. Take special care around her eyes, which are vulnerable to infection in the early days. Tear cotton balls into small pieces. Wet and squeeze out the excess. Wipe once with each piece, going in only one direction, from the nose outward.

7. The final step is the shampoo. With the baby lying on her back, hold her head in your hand, resting her body on your forearm. (Her bottom and legs should rest on the bathing surface.) Hold her head over the pan. Dip the washcloth in the

water, squeeze most of it out and use the cloth to dampen her hair. Repeat until her hair is thoroughly wet. Squeeze a drop or two of baby shampoo on your fingers (this is a one-handed trick you can practice), or you can pre-measure a little into the bottle cap. Gently massage her scalp and hair. Rinse as before. Gently towel dry.

AN OLDER BABY can be bathed lying on her bath sponge in a sink or tub with two inches of water, using the same list of accessories. Be sure the room is warm and use soap sparingly, if at all. Encourage her to kick and play in the water. You can dip your washcloth in the water and squeeze it on her belly. She'll be amazed at the sensation!

ONCE AGAIN, NEVER LEAVE YOUR BABY DURING BATH TIME!

BOTTLE-FEEDING

If your baby is bottle-fed, you can share the joy (and exhaustion) of feeding times. You can derive real pleasure in giving her the nourishment she wants and needs. You may choose the early morning and the just-before-bedtime bottles as your special time with her. Be sure to help with the daily bottle cleaning and formula preparation as often as possible. It's only fair that you share the chores as well as the fun.

A Personal Challenge

The father's dual role of nurturer/provider is a challenging one. Be prepared to discover some difficulties in reconciling the two. You will almost certainly be caught up in it the moment you start thinking about providing for your new family. There's a tender new life in your charge, someone completely dependent on you for food, clothing and shelter, not to mention the truckload of money needed for a college education.

ANOTHER BOTTLE POSITION

The traditional method of feeding a baby a bottle is to hold her head nestled in the crook of your arm, with her body lying along your arm.

Here's an alternative that promotes eye contact and helps her learn your face and its expressions while she drinks:

Sitting down with your legs together and your feet propped on a low stool, lie the baby along the niche created by your legs. Her head should be elevated by your knees, her legs curled up naturally into your lap.

You would be in a tiny minority if you didn't feel that you must work harder, to earn more, to "get ahead," so that you can build a better future for your new family. If your wife stays home, you lose her income. If she returns to work, you will still have a tremendous responsibility to shoulder (and expensive babysitting fees to pay). If you yourself work at home, you may find yourself becoming the primary caregiver—but the need for a babysitter will still be there.

Whatever your decision, you'll want to plan for your family's future. Make sure that the steps you take are rooted in common sense. For example, take out a life insurance that you can afford and open a savings plan—however small—to get you started. You can increase the amounts of both later on.

Being a good provider is a noble ambition. It also poses a profound dilemma if you want to be a hands-on father, rather than an absentee. How to do both is problematical: Working hard takes you away from your baby. You may not want to observe your baby from beyond the barricade of your job. Though your job may take you away from your baby during the day, you can use the time when you are home to nurture—and play with—her.

Though in some cases men have stayed home while their partners returned to work, most men don't opt to be house-husbands. In a two-career household it is more likely that either your wife will stay home for a while or you will both return to work. If both of you are going back to work, you will then need to enlist the

NURTURING BY OTHERS

If your wife plans to go back to work after your baby comes, you will need to decide on the kind of care she should have. Quality of care, affordability and convenience are the most important points to consider in making your choice. As you look into the resources in your area, you will probably find these options:

In-Home Care

Hiring someone to come to your home to care for your baby is expensive but convenient. Your baby has a one-on-one relationship with her caregiver, remains in the environment she is accustomed to, and is less likely to catch colds and other illnesses from other children.

The best sources of candidates for the job are domestic employment agencies, word of mouth, and advertising in the newspaper. Prescreen each applicant over the phone and then interview the best candidates in person. Make sure your baby is there to meet each one. Note carefully how they handle her and how she reacts to them. If you are in doubt, keep looking.

Out-of-Home Care

There are two basic kinds of out-of-home care: day-care centers and family-care homes. A day-care center cares for a number of children in an institutional atmosphere. Family care is a less formal arrangement in which a woman, often with young children of her own, cares for a few others in return for a reasonable daily or weekly fee.

In a good family-care home your baby will receive quality care and learn how to cope with other children. A good day-care center can be as expensive as in-home care. But it may be worth the expense because it offers a wide range of stimulating activities, professional staff and, of course, other children to play with.

The best sources of out-of-home care are local child-care referral services and word of mouth. If you are exploring options in your area, examine each for health, cleanliness and quality of care. Interview each extensively before making a choice and afterward constantly monitor your baby's situation.

help of a competent caregiver to raise your baby while you are away.

Fathering is a plus equation. Think of all it can add to your life—wider and deeper emotional range; satisfaction and pride at proving you can do it; new accomplishments, sensitivities, responsiveness, generosity; an expanded sense of meaning, significance and purpose.

As you share the joy and the work of raising a family, you'll hold your baby, rock her, play with her; give her as much of your time, and yourself, as you can. Lying on your chest, she will have the best naps of her life. You and she will get to know each other, and you will belong to each other.

5

Keeping Your Relationship on Track

C hildbirth affects you and your wife in different and often opposite ways. During pregnancy your wife has been the center of attention. With any sort of luck, everyone has been solicitous of her health and mental state, and mindful of the ordeal yet to come. Now that she has completed her initial assignment, the focus—yours and everyone else's—switches to the baby. In her mind's eye the baby's mother loses her special status. A couple of days after childbirth, she will fall into what's commonly known as postpartum blues.

Not only does she lose her position in the spotlight, she may have a stomach that hasn't snapped back to its original shape, and the irritating pain of stitches (if she has had a cesarean birth, her discomfort is on a much higher level—she's recovering from abdominal surgery).

Your experience, on the other hand, is the reverse. You're on the receiving end. All at once, your baby, whom you could not approach or know before, is given to you. You'll need to appreciate that your gain is your wife's loss and that she may compensate for this by doting possessively on her infant, particularly if she breast-feeds him.

Avoid joining in a tug-of-war with her. The baby must not be a prize to fight over. If you do, everybody loses, including the baby. If anything will save the day, it is communication. Talk

A GESTURE IS WORTH A THOUSAND WORDS

Sometimes it is difficult to say what you mean. When words fail, touch takes over. Embrace your partner and your baby in your arms. Holding them close makes a clear, bold statement of intent that would melt the stoniest heart.

So what if the nurse may walk into the hospital room. This time belongs to the three of you, and the intimacy of it should not be spoiled by inhibitions. Getting off on the right foot is essential. You will create a memory bank that you and your wife can draw on for strength, comfort and encouragement in the difficult early days.

over your feelings. Give your wife the attention and affection she needs.

Opening your heart and sharing feelings with her will help you both to move past the conflict of mother/baby vs. father/baby. Give and take will help the three of you come together.

Sharing the Workload

There is a myth floating about that being home with a baby, in and of itself, is a wonderful experience. But babies require repeated, extensive attention that can become tiresome. Parents on the front line need to escape from their demanding little charges. If they don't get away, what start out as acts of loving care can turn into joyless exercises—or worse. The pleasure of tending baby can become soured by the arid vista of never-ending diapering, feeding, bathing, soothing . . . . Burnout is a distinct possibility.

If your wife perceives that she is shouldering the nurturing burden alone, she is likely to be resentful. After all, *you* get to go out into the real world and talk to *real* people. *She's* stuck at home up to her elbows in formula and baby wash. Though by working you take on the all-important provider role—without you, she and the baby would be, quite literally, cold, homeless and hungry—your wife will still begrudge you all the "fun" you find in the outside world.

It is important to work side by side with your wife. If she is at home with the baby during the day, you should be prepared to take on baby duty as soon as you come home. She will welcome relief, particularly if you arrive at the witching hours of early evening. You are fresh (even though tired from work), ready for baby battle; she is weary, ready for reinforcements.

Think of it as tag-team parenting. When one of you is fed up with the baby (and as he grows older, and the "Terrible Twos" set in, you will know just what that means), you hand off the baby like a baton. The parent gets a break to recoup and return again.

Sharing the care of your baby will boost your adult relationship as well.

Talking together, you can share your feelings about the baby. If you chip in and help out, you will be better equipped to understand *her* feelings. Additionally, your help with the baby reinforces the unity of your tiny family. When you bathe, feed and diaper him, you'll be saying to your wife that you're in this together, and that you take nothing for granted.

This is powerful medicine for calming the emotional stress you're both going through, and will add new, rich dimensions to your relationship.

Jealousy

It will also lay the groundwork for dealing with an emotion that may take you by surprise because it seems so unreasonable, even obnoxious, under the circumstances. That emotion is jealousy.

Here's how it commonly happens. You observe how completely self-enclosed and seemingly natural together your wife and baby are. They're like one person. You look enviously on this closeness and wonder if you can ever attain such an intimacy with your child. You feel you're at a disadvantage because you go to work. It seems unfair.

More disturbing is the way the baby can take over your wife. You're losing the private space with her that once was exclusively yours; he has appropriated it. Intimate moments, quiet times, when you and your partner could shut out the world, are up for grabs, and baby takes all. Despite your deepest longings you often feel you're an outsider, and you don't want to be outside either wife or baby. The hateful word "rejection" crowds out more positive emotions and thoughts.

Of course the baby makes a difference in your relationship with your wife. With a third person added to your life, particularly a helpless, dependent one, you can't expect business as usual. Hard as that may be to accept, it's perfectly natural.

The first step is to explore your feelings with your wife. Ignored or buried, they'll fester and poison the relationship. She'll understand negative feelings. She has them too. You have been companions and lovers. No more than you does she want to lose something that is as invaluable to her as it is to you.

Grandparents Are Free

What's needed at this moment is for the two of you to change the details of your relationship so that they match the change your baby has introduced. The solution isn't difficult, but it does take joint, planned effort.

Call it time-out from parenting, *your* time, *quality* time. You need the opportunity to recover the sense that you and your wife are people with needs and emotions of your own as well as responsible parents of a little baby.

Reserve one or two days a week when you two can plan to go out for dinner and a movie or stay in for a sexual evening. What you crave now are relaxing, private interludes. A couple of hours two times a week will do wonders for your morale and your relationship.

Find sitters who can be retained on a regular basis. Pay them extra to keep them loyal. Grandparents (are free), referrals from a domestic service, an ad in the paper or yellow pages, or a neighborly widow are all sources of babysitting services. With the exception of grandparents, in-depth interviews filled with "what if" questions are strongly recommended.

To simplify the time it takes to plan your nights out, it may work to schedule Wednesday and Saturday evenings. With a phone call or two, you can make arrangements for your evenings out a month at a time. Don't worry about the cost. Remember: Babysitters are cheaper than psychiatrists!

This means time away from your baby, a prospect that may

make you and your wife uncomfortable. This infant, both before birth and since, has absorbed massive amounts of your attention and energies, and without realizing it you've built a wall around your existence with him. You're not sure you can move outside it. But you *have* to. You and your wife risk emotional suffocation if you don't let fresh air into the cloistered environment of parenting.

Sexual Relations

During the six-week postpartum period, when you and your partner abstain from sex, she becomes daily more desirable to you. While you are waiting out this period, there are sexually gratifying alternatives to full lovemaking that you can adopt, and she can experience orgasm without running any risk of physical harm.

Once this period is behind you and you're back on the lovemaking track, you probably won't be surprised that it runs along a much different route from before. The reason, of course, is the presence of your baby. His demands for attention are likely to interrupt your lovemaking or may leave you both so exhausted that sleep is preferable to sex.

Unfortunately, there's another problem that can sabotage conjugal bliss. Don't be disappointed or disillusioned if sexual desire revives in her at a slower pace than you would like. It takes time for the radical physical changes that occurred in her during pregnancy to shift back to normal. In addition to nature, real-life adjustment to mothering takes its toll as well. Up with the baby during the night and going nonstop all day, she's tired. And if she's nursing, hormonal activity makes her even more tired.

Luckily, this period won't last. As the baby sleeps through the night with regularity (it varies from baby to baby, the average is at about six months), you and she will be more rested.

Taking Over

We have said that daily duties that you get into the habit of doing are important. But what about your days off? Think about taking over the baby duty so that your wife can have part or all of a day to herself. (If she is nursing, she will obviously still have to do that piece of the work.) You will get to know your baby and she will have the break she needs.

This plan may not be simple to implement if your wife feels proprietary about the baby. To her, caring for him means more than executing a clutch of physical tasks; it enables her to fulfill her image of the mother role. These day-to-day activities can be a mirror in which your wife may read, and measure, her maternal performance. Lots of profound emotions may be at work here.

Taking over will be easier if you discuss your intentions before the baby comes and start doing baby duty from Day One. If you learn your way around the nursery together, *and do it with a sense of humor,* then you start off even. If she stays home with the baby and you go back to work after the baby is born, she will necessarily learn more about baby care. You will have to cram into off-work hours what she has all day to do.

Talking over your role as a nurturing father before the baby is born sets the stage for give-and-take later on. If she agrees beforehand that she is going to share the baby's care with you, there will be fewer emotional firestorms once the star of the show has arrived. As the baby settles in at home, you can adapt your baby chores to fit your schedule and your wife's needs.

As we have said before, don't compete for *"Best Parent."*

Reprise

As you read this guide to becoming a father, it may seem that we've set out an endless obstacle course for you to run. It has been nothing but do this here, give more there, don't complain, be patient, it will all be worth it in the end. You leap one hurdle and there's another one ahead of you, and the promised land seems as insubstantial as smoke.

The trouble with language, a great writer once said, is that it's only words. Well, unfortunately, language is all we have to tell you about the tremendous benefits of exploring the role of father, of growing into it. A film you see, or the sight of friends in action with their babies, may contribute immediacy, but they're still only words made visible.

The bottom-line truth is that you can't be a father ahead of time any more than you can be in love before it happens. Chances are you'll be a better father, and lover, by having some advance understanding of what to expect from each experience, of where the pitfalls are and how to avoid them—or extricate yourself if you happen to stumble into one.

But when it comes to the extraordinary difference that nurturing and loving a baby can make in your life, there's no alchemy that can turn plain words into gold. You can't know the difference until you try it.

Doing is believing.

Believe.

PART II

WATCHING YOUR BABY GROW

As a new father, you have entered the realm of Babyhood. Like Alice in Wonderland, you discover a world where magic is performed and wondrous transformations appear. Your baby's accomplishments start small, with lungs that breathe and eyes that focus. Soon, these are followed by hands that grasp and smiles that repay your rapt attention. And as with so many transformations in nature, no amount of looking can prepare you for the magic that takes place when the parts come together to form something greater than their sum. Before you know it your baby is neither a baby nor even a toddler—he is a child running into school with his backpack trailing behind.

It happens fast but it doesn't happen easily. Each milestone is a tribute to human tenacity and parental patience. At first glance your baby's movements may look random or purposeless. But they aren't. His urge to grow up is inescapable. He invests all his waking energy in learning and doing. He takes advantage of accidental success, uses trial and error to find his way. Every big accomplishment is the result of a string of small ones. The end result is indeed remarkable.

As he struggles with the work of growing up, you have to stay close by, making sure he's safe, comforting him when he falls and cheering him on. Parenting is a demanding job. Joy and wonder exchange places with despair and exhaustion on a daily basis. As a father you are in for quite a roller-coaster ride. But you wouldn't have it any other way. How else would you be privy to the miracle of life?

Think of the following chapters as sections of a map that points out landmarks of development and guides you through each turn and dip of babyhood and the early toddler period. Knowing the guideposts will help you relax and enjoy your baby's trip through infancy.

6

Breaking the Mold

Four on the Floor

FIRST, MEET ALEXANDER

On his first birthday he is very tall for his age, bald and round, if not downright fat. The Michelin man rolls on his arms and thighs don't seem to hinder his mobility. He has been crawling for five months now. He is steady on his feet and is on the verge of walking. It is hard to explain his extra pounds. He doesn't overeat, nor does his mother overfeed him. The pediatrician assures his parents that he will probably slim down in the coming year. He gets bored with toys easily, moving from one to another in rapid succession. He is quick to show frustration if he can't open a container or fit a peg into a hole.

Now, at age five, Alexander is beautifully proportioned and weighs exactly the right amount. He is passionate about playing and watching sports. His ability is better than average, but he's no superstar. He shows terrible frustration when trying to write letters of the alphabet or coloring within the lines. Though often angry with himself, he shows a sensitivity to other people's feelings and is quietly shy around people outside the family circle. He is the oldest child in his family and his parents perhaps expect too much of him.

NOW, HERE'S CHRISTOPHER

At 14 months he is very tall and very skinny. He has always been so. Legs and arms like toothpicks. The pediatrician has assured his mother that it is much better to be "lean and mean than tall and fat. He eats well, and that's what matters." At a time when most of his contemporaries are mobile, Christopher shows no interest in walking. He crawls nicely and seems to see no reason to get up. He is much more interested in his toys and will sit for hours surrounded by them, inspecting each in turn. Earlier, when he was seven months old, he was eager to learn to sit up on his own, perhaps so that he could free his hands to play with his toys. As Christopher is the second child in the family, his parents are less worried and more relaxed about his development.

Today, at age five, Christopher is filling out. He is still tall and thin, but he doesn't look so fragile. He loves projects, the bigger and more complicated the better. His concentration is powerful. He tunes out the rest of the world (including the voices of his parents) as he focuses on his work. He enjoys playing and watching sports. Unlike the boys on the pickup soccer team who merely follow the ball around, he has a sense of strategy and how to play his position.

NEXT, MEET MARY

She is very small at ten months, light as a feather, with big brown eyes and curly auburn hair. She is precocious. She has already begun to walk, shows a keen interest in talking and loves to listen to all sorts of words and sounds. Indeed, she seems to share her parents' love of classical music. She cut her first tooth listening to the music of Bach, Mozart and Beethoven.

When her professional pianist mommy sits with her at the keyboard of their Steinway grand, Mary can finger the keys. Her parents are bursting their buttons over their first child and love to boast to friends that she is something special.

Today, at age five, Mary can read, stay within the lines of a coloring book and she chooses her colors carefully. She's been taking piano lessons for two years and can play several pieces. Her athletic ability is unremarkable and her interest in physical activity is almost nil. Her parents try to encourage her to be more active but have only been able to get her to ice skate a little.

FINALLY, HERE'S JOANNA

She's a pistol, this one. At 14 months she is strong, built like a fireplug and never stops moving. She has been walking for months and now runs headlong around the house after her two older brothers, aged 7 and 5, ready for any roughhousing game. She loves to play ball with them—when they have the patience and interest to stoop to her level. She shows athletic promise far beyond her age. Form boards and pop-it beads lie on the toy shelf virtually untouched. She's much more interested in her older brothers' toys and eager to "help" them. Joanna's parents have their hands full keeping the peace among the children, and diverting their daughter from the older boys' board games and electric train set.

Now, at age five, Joanna has slimmed down some, though you would still probably call her chunky. She has stayed with her tomboy interests and is usually one of the first to be chosen for a team. But she has also expanded her world to include a few dolls and delights in setting tea for them, using old plastic cups and saucers from the kitchen. She uses her mother's old dishes because the doll-sized ones aren't real. As the youngest of three, she is in a hurry to grow up and enjoy the freedom her brothers have. She struggles when dressing herself because buttons and snaps are difficult to manage. But her mind-set is determined and she will prevail. Because she is the "baby" of the family and the only girl, her parents tend to shelter her—which she finds irritating.

These children are four examples of human lives at the beginning. They will go on to school, a first love, a job and perhaps a family of their own. If it were possible to sketch every person born in the past, present and future, each would be quite different. Each person responds to his or her world at any given time with a unique viewpoint and capability.

The catalog of human possibilities is an endless book without a front or back cover. Every baby has an individual matrix of variables, like personality, ability and interest, which will help determine the path of development which he or she will take throughout life. How adept or agile the baby is will hinge on the inner workings of these variables. It is a matter of degree, not kind. Every normal baby learns to walk, talk and manipulate objects.

Great Expectations

But development doesn't occur in a vacuum. The parents of the four children in our thumbnail sketches greatly influence the way their offspring grow up. All parents do. It is awesome to consider that you are in some measure responsible for your baby's making the most of her potential. You provide stimulation. You provide the environment, both physical and emotional, that enables her to stretch as far as she can. Throughout this section, we will be talking a lot about environmental quality on both levels and how you can achieve it.

Unfortunately, parents often impart negative feelings to their children as well. They are usually carrying a fair amount of emotional baggage with them as they enter parenting and, unconsciously, they saddle their children with some of it. Babies pick up bad vibrations very easily. Parents can be anxious and insecure, or filled with preset ideas about who their baby will be or what she will do. Beware of expecting too much of her or of yourself. You will end up worrying and feeling guilty or disappointed when reality doesn't match your dream. Remember that your baby is her own person. *She is not either one of you.*

These days parents invest a huge amount of emotional capital in their babies. In earlier times, families were large and the risks were great that children would die young, many of them before the age of two. Most parents today can confidently expect their new babies to be healthy and to continue to be so as they grow up. They have fewer children and look for a great deal of fulfillment from those they have. Wanting to give the best and the most to their baby, they in turn want little Sally or Paul to develop apace. In the business world it would be known as a return on investment. In the baby's small world it just may not be possible.

This Is Not the Army

A baby has her own internal schedule for development, which is uniquely her own. That may bother you. It is too nebulous. The specific structure of a timetable is much more appealing. If she does what an expert says, you can feel reassured. Such a schedule helps you gauge how things are going and compare your baby to a uniform standard of ability and achievement.

If you are anxious about your baby's progress, a timetable goes a long way to allay your fears. When she performs on or ahead of schedule, you can point with assurance and pride. But what if she doesn't follow the book? (After all, she can't read it!) You leave yourself open to a trap. Many babies don't do what they are supposed to *when they are supposed to.*

At this point, the emotional environmental quality act kicks in. Your first impulse may be to push your baby ahead. Resist it. This is not a dog-sled race with you wielding the whip; instead, be a supportive coach. Your encouragement, your cheering her on, will help your child move from one achievement to the next.

As hard as it may seem, your job as a parent is to relax and enjoy watching your baby learn. It will help you if you stop and think about what she has already accomplished and what lies ahead. But remember it is her game and *she* decides what to try for next. Don't worry about the order of business; she'll get there. After all, how often do you meet a four-year-old who can't walk, talk or maneuver toys? Once you take the pressure off, both you and she will feel much better.

Unfortunately, this is easier said than done. As new parents you are constantly evaluating your baby's progress by comparing her to other babies. It is almost irresistible. You gravitate to others with new babies, knowing that they'll be interested in the topic that so consumes you. In the park, at cocktail parties, over the fence, conversation inevitably turns to a discussion of the progress of the babies. All is well if your baby is on schedule.

But what if she's not? Seeing or hearing about babies who conform or are ahead of schedule can shake you up. There is a good deal of one-upmanship in the social intercourse of new parents: You can be sure you'll hear *all* about little Jonathan's first steps, particularly if your little Janie is still on her hands and knees.

You Gotta Believe

It may be hard to feel confident walking on the spongy ground of "every baby's different," but you have prestigious experts in the field of baby development cheering you on. One of the foremost of these is T. Berry Brazelton, M.D., whose theory about active, quiet and average babies is discussed in some detail below.

Parents are often reluctant to let their baby be herself and find her own way. It usually takes time for them to realize, at first hand, that babies do end up walking, talking and doing things for themselves. As second-time-around parents, you'll be smarter about that. As you and your partner take your first trip through parenting, expert advice from your pediatrician and other medical advisers will help ease your minds.

All Things Large and Small

A baby's efforts to master her body fall into two basic categories: large motor and small motor control. The large muscles in this tiny body must learn the basics of sitting, walking, running and throwing a ball. Separately, the small muscles must work together to grasp and manipulate objects, handling large, simple things at first, but graduating to smaller and more complicated objects as skills increase. As the baby perfects large and small skills, she will be able to do them together.

While each baby has her own internal schedule, there is a general sequence to track as she grows: Development moves downward, starting at her head, then moving to her trunk and finally to her legs and feet. Similarly, her upper arms must be under control before her fingers and thumbs can do their job. Development over these two years is an enormous task, one that we may have trouble comprehending because we can't remember learning it ourselves. A baby must gain control of her body and master difficult feats of balance, strength and dexterity.

And that's only the beginning. She must unravel the mysteries of the world she's suddenly fallen into. She must make order out of chaos. She has to catalog the noises that fill her ears and the objects that dance before her eyes. Her hands must discover and chart the tangible world. She has to connect all three together before going any further.

Normal Is Different

Experts agree that "normal" has a very broad scope. Some babies walk at nine months, others at 15 months. (Six months is a wide range in the short time span of babyhood.) Babies themselves decide the order of motor skills they will learn and differ in the speed with which they learn them.

For example, a baby who creeps around may learn to stand up, then think better of it and drop down on all fours and crawl about for awhile to get in some horizontal practice before working on upright locomotion. Then when she has determined that the time is right, she will get up and finish the work she began weeks before. In addition, she may switch her interest from large muscle activity over to small muscle tasks, and then return after a week or a month to where she left off in her large muscle assignment.

As your baby progresses, she will often reach plateaus of motor growth, punctuated by spurts of progress. At first the flatter part of the curve may seem like a lull in achievement, but if you look closer, you are likely to see that she is not idle. She is intently refining and perfecting skills just learned. The length of the pause will depend on her individual internal clock.

Active, Quiet and In-Between

According to Brazelton, a normal baby may be very active, very quiet or anywhere between the two extremes. At one end are the babies who never stop moving, who can exhaust even a top Olympic athlete. (Olympian great Jim Thorpe once imitated the exhaustive motions of an infant and quit. The baby kept going!) Relentless exercising propels an active baby's large motor development far ahead of other, more sedate babies.

ACTIVE BABIES

These go-go babies are constantly trying to enlarge their repertoire of gross motor skills. Because a baby like this is so immersed in large muscle movements, she pays less attention to her smaller muscles. The heroic effort she makes is obvious and visible to her parents, who rarely worry about their baby's progress, even if her hand-eye coordination is slow. It is clear to these parents that their baby is giving it her all. Rightly enough, they reason that their athlete baby will concentrate on small motor control when the first tasks are accomplished.

Life for an active baby is filled with bumps and bruises. Mom and Dad may spend a lot of time kissing better the Lumps and Owies gotten along the way. Other active babies have a higher pain threshold and careen from one spill to the next with only minor protests of discomfort. When an active baby becomes mobile, she often gets into trouble and she will lead everyone on a merry chase throughout her babyhood.

QUIET BABIES

At the other extreme are the quiet babies, the look-and-listen ones, who drink in their environment, digesting and exploring the sensory world. Quiet babies learn to manipulate smallish objects much earlier than their active brothers and sisters. They are alive to nuances, fingering shapes and textures, alert to subtleties of noise and the visual patterns that surround them. These babies tend to develop long attention spans which boost their abilities to learn later on in school.

As you can imagine, the quiet baby lacks the shoot-'em-up showmanship of the active baby. She is too busy with hand coordination to be interested in wowing her folks with feats of accomplishment. Because of this lack of action, parents of quiet babies tend to worry because their baby "just lies there." Inevitably, she

QUIET BABY STRATEGY

Woe to the parents who try to push their baby into action. They will have very little luck. The baby may actively resist any attempt to put her in a seated or standing position. Her body may stiffen rigidly or her legs may fold uselessly when she is forced to stand.

While pushing is definitely out, encouragement is in. You can entice her to move forward by putting a favorite toy just out of reach. (Make sure it is a toy she really likes or the experiment will fail.) If she is on her tummy on the floor, put it on the floor beyond her grasp. If she is standing up, but reluctant to walk, hold the toy in your hand and suggest she come and get it.

Failed attempts easily discourage her, so you must be careful. Encourage her inch by inch, when she has a reasonable chance of success. Break down each task into its smallest pieces and let her build up slowly to each crescendo of accomplishment. Offer a safety net to catch her if she falls.

For example, suppose your baby loves to hold and examine a variety of objects, but is reluctant to learn how to sit independently. Take her on a grocery run and put her into the child seat of a grocery cart. Tie a large belt or wide scarf around her middle and the metal spokes of the seat. Stuff a blanket or your jacket around her. As you stroll the aisles, ply her with tins and boxes (things edible and nonbreakable only, please) to examine, bang and shake. Watch carefully that she doesn't eat the wrappings of the items you hand her. Teach her to hand things back when she is ready for something new.

(This trick has a built-in bonus: At the end of the lesson, you've done the family's grocery shopping!)

---

falls behind more active competitors in the large motor contest. Anxious parents become concerned because their baby compares unfavorably with other babies they see.

A sedate, quiet baby will finally make her move into the world of large muscle activity, but in her own good time. Her first attempts will be tentative, inching forward on her belly. As she progresses in large muscle development, she will probably be cautious and easily daunted by her failed attempts.

IN-BETWEEN BABIES

In the middle of the spectrum we find the average baby, who does a bit of this and a bit of that, alternately choosing chores from both large and small muscle development "to-do" lists. This in-between baby alternates between quiet and active moods. Some of the time she delights her parents with infant acrobatics; at other times she is calm and receptive to her environment. In the downward head-to-toe trend of development discussed earlier, she will fall in the middle of a timetable laid out by experts, neither slow nor fast, in both large and small muscle categories.

The route an in-between baby takes to the finish line will be uniquely her own. Don't be fooled by the word "average." It doesn't mean dull!

Each Baby to Her Own

On the continuum from the active baby to the quiet baby, every normal child carves her own niche, reinventing the wheel each time. Remember the quartet who opened this chapter? A baby brings into the world a specific predisposition to a certain type of behavior, a kind of pattern, which is your first gift to her at conception.

Your role as parents is to nurture and encourage this bundle of genes, giving full rein to her potential. (Parents of very active babies may find a harness more appropriate for their needs!) What you cannot do, even if you wanted to, is to change how she develops.

If your baby is quiet and slow to get moving, you may be uneasy. You see other babies on the go and doing things you wish your baby would also do. Remember—she is a person in her own right whose potential is different from others. Perhaps she is not going to be a star athlete, but she might well be a creative or intellectual giant. Whoever she is, with your love and help she will be the best she can be.

Now that we have a firm grip on the variety of life and the

babies who keep it going, we will sketch in the chapters ahead an outline of how babies grow, tracking the overall progress of large and small muscle control, as well as personal and cultural adjustment.

We are wanted now at the starting line, where your newborn is waiting for us, ready to get on with the exciting business of life.

7

Getting Started

"A baby is God's opinion that the world should continue."
—ANONYMOUS

If we take this old saying to heart and extend the idea, we can also say that newborn reflexes are the tools God gives each baby to survive his adjustment to the outside world.

Consider some specifics. Without a moment of hesitation, soon after birth, your baby's mouth sucks when his cheek is stroked, ready to eat for the first time. Totally helpless, he grasps your finger tightly, holding on for dear life. With the aid of a gag reflex, he can help clear his own lungs of the mucus left over from his days in the womb, which he needs to get rid of so that he can breathe properly.

In his own little way your newborn can protect himself from the world around him. His eyelids blink strongly shut to protect his eyes from too much light or other unwanted stimuli. To avoid smothering, he will twist his head from side to side to escape whatever is over his nose and mouth. If this maneuver fails, he then crosses his arms over his face to knock it off. Furthermore, he can react to pain by pulling himself away and then trying to push the source of it away.

Reflexes also show that your newborn has a preliminary "knowledge" of crawling, walking and even swimming, thoughtfully preset before birth. Lying on his tummy, he will respond to pressure on his foot and crawl forward, unaware that he is moving through space. He may even rise up on his arms as he hurtles

LIFE ON THE INSIDE

Close your eyes and imagine what it is like to be curled up in the warm, cozy, watery womb before birth. The sun never rises here. It is dark and quiet except for the thumping sound of your mother's heartbeat, the gurgling of her stomach and the distant, muffled sounds of the outside world. You don't need to breathe. You've never been hungry, nor can you eat, for that matter.

You are confined to quarters. You can't move from one place to another. Space has no meaning: There is no up and down, forward or reverse, front and back, or side . . . .

Now it is time to leave. Hours later, after being pressed and squeezed through the birth canal, you arrive bruised and battered. Suddenly there is light and air. If you don't fill your lungs and cry, a slap on your bottom or feet will start you off smartly.

As a newborn you are trying to cope with a myriad sensations. The world you have suddenly fallen into is strange. For the first time you feel texture against your skin. Hunger now drives you to learn to suck for your food. You are carried around, picked up and put down, handled this way and that. You feel your limbs move through the air. As yet, you have no idea who or what is around you or why.

Amazing things happen to a baby in the beginning. Give him calm. It is what he needs most.

forward. For a few days after birth, the baby takes automatic steps on a surface, whenever he is stood up and his foot pressed down. In water he makes swimming motions, though he has no idea how to swim.

Not every reflexive movement has obvious usefulness. But some are remarkably valuable to the new baby trying to make his way in life. The tonic neck reflex is one of these. In it, the baby, lying on his back, turns his head to one side or the other and arranges his arms in a fencer's stance, i.e. extending the arm in front of his face and flexing the other behind his head. This reflexive arm and head position helps the baby in two ways, by requiring him to use each side of his body and encouraging him to focus his eyes on his hands. Both are important boosts in the development task ahead.

One of the most dramatic involuntary responses, called the Moro reflex, is the startle reaction to sudden noise or contact. Your baby when disturbed drops his head back, flings out his arms and legs sharply, and begins crying. The sound of his own crying startles him again and a vicious cycle is established. (Steady pressure on a part of his body will help break the chain.) Though the Moro reflex is an involuntary signal, it is also an effective way of communicating with those around him. You get the message loud and clear: Handle Me With Care!

Most reflexive responses disappear after awhile, some more quickly than others. A few, like the stepping, creeping and swimming reflexes, reappear later as controlled voluntary behavior. Others, like coughing, yawning and sneezing, stay with us all through our lives. Traces of others remain as well: The tonic neck reflex often shows up in the posture of a sleeping adult; the Moro reflex can be seen in the reaction of a startled adult.

Getting Control: The First Three Months

As your baby grows, he has less need for the reflexes that were so vital in the beginning. Development progresses and he gradu-

---

SMILING

The first time your baby smiles at you is truly a memorable event. It is particularly important to parents, because it is their first recognizable emotional connection with this new, rather disorganized human being. For weeks they have been losing sleep and dedicating their lives to the well-being of their new baby. Now finally comes the reward.

A baby's first smile of recognition varies depending on individual development. Babies practice fleeting pseudo-smiles almost from birth. You probably won't see the real thing in direct response to your voice and face until the second month begins.

---

ally takes control of his body. As we said earlier, his efforts begin with his head and travel south. Your baby will choose his own order of events: He may emphasize either the large or the small muscles, or perhaps he will mix and match the two.

BABY'S HEAD

Your newborn's head is huge and too heavy for his tiny body to handle. It wobbles and drops if unsupported in the air. Just imagine how you would manage if your head was as heavy as a bowling ball! Like any athlete in training he must build up his neck and back muscles in order to hold it up properly. When he is lying on his tummy you will see him practice: He will turn his nose to the mattress and then turn to rest on his cheek. As he gains strength, he will lift his head for a few seconds when his nose reaches the midway point. The length of time he can manage will increase with practice. By the end of three months, he will be able to lift his head for several minutes.

As these muscles strengthen, your baby will be able to sit supported in your lap or be held parallel to the ground, and work at holding his head up. These feats are harder to do than the head lifts he did earlier on his tummy. Gravity's pull increases when he is held upright or held without a supporting surface, causing his head to bob. With practice he will hold his head steadier.

On his back, he gains control of turning his head. At three months he will keep his head in midposition (ending the tonic neck reflex) and perhaps be able to lift it up off the bed.

LARGE MUSCLES

When your baby gains control of his head and upper torso, he can begin to concentrate on the motions of his arms and legs. In contrast to the jerky movements of a younger baby, he can now cycle and wave his arms and legs alternately in a constant, smooth rhythm.

HAND-EYE COORDINATION

A quiet baby shines in this department. The tight reflexive grasp opens up during these three months. Your baby has "found" his

CURTAIN ROD MOBILE: A CHANGEABLE FEAST

As soon as you settle your baby at home, it is time to think about practical ways to stimulate him while you are near but doing something else. Before he is able to sit up, he'll be content to lie on his back and play in his crib or playpen.

To that end you can rig an easy home-made mobile: Take an expandable curtain rod, *one with curved ends,* to hook over the sides of his crib or playpen (a straight rod could fall into the crib and hurt the baby). Using secure knots, tie large, smooth objects like measuring spoons or cups (without the metal ring that holds them together) with strong string. Select objects that make noise when they are disturbed. If they are brightly colored or patterned, so much the better. Change the toys at least twice a week and always remove the mobile when you leave the room.

Suggested Household Items

- Embroidery hoops (different sizes)
- Measuring spoons and cups (as above)
- Plastic dime store bracelets (plain)
- Napkin rings (plain)
- Baby cup and feeding spoon (silver makes a lovely sound)

Look around the house for items that are appropriate. Just make sure they are nontoxic and won't flake, break or poke him when he learns to grab and eat them. You can put favorite rattles on the mobile as well.

BONUS POINT: If you hang a large stuffed animal or other soft colorful object on the mobile by itself and put it down by his feet, you'll encourage him to bang at it with his feet. This will help his walking motions when he gets up on his feet months down the road.

hands, and watches them move for long periods of time. He brings them to his mouth and then extends them back into the range of vision. He begins to understand that his hands are an extension of himself, not an object outside himself.

SIGHT AND SOUND

SEEING: At birth your baby will focus for a couple of seconds on something eight inches away. He "notices" it. Anything further away is blurry. As he matures, his field of vision expands (at four months he will have adult acuity) and his attention span lengthens.

Research shows that babies are more interested in human faces and face-like patterns and look at those longer than at other patterns or objects. It should be no surprise that your baby is most interested in the face he sees most often and recognizes that one first. Usually it's a Mommy face with Daddy coming a very close second.

HEARING: Sudden loud sounds startle young babies, while gentle, continuous sounds like music are soothing to them. In the same way that faces attract attention, the human voice has irresistible appeal. Of all the voices that your baby hears, he works hardest to identify one or two that are most important to him, and most likely they are the voices of his mother and father.

When your baby connects a face with a voice, the stage is set for social interaction. His first friends are the two of you. As weeks go by, he expands the number of voices and faces he knows, to include siblings or grandparents.

As soon as your baby discovers his hands and opens his fingers, he learns to get hold of an object in his hand voluntarily. His early attempts at reaching and grabbing are clumsy. Presented with an object within his reach, he bats it with a closed fist. At first he misses the target, but soon he will hit it more often. He will also try another strategy: to reach for an object with both hands. Practice will improve his aim and grasp. Awkwardness will melt away.

Personal Relations

During the first weeks your baby's main avenue of communication is crying. For reasons best known to him, he may well choose the early evening hour to split the air with his wailing, just when you want to sit down for a quiet meal with your partner. You may find you have to take turns holding him while dinner is a) being made, and b) being eaten.

In the next two months he cries less and learns to express himself in other ways. In turn he coos, whimpers, chortles, gurgles and squeals with frustration.

He responds differently to each of his parents. "Mother" has a special status. Your baby is actively interested in his mother's comings and goings, and if she leaves the room, he may cry in protest.

Gradually your baby widens his circle of familiar people. He turns his head (as he gains the control mentioned earlier) to watch and listen to what they are doing and may vocalize when they talk to him.

Cultural Habits

Earlier in this chapter we highlighted the major adjustments your newborn must make. Everything is new to him, he is disorganized and he will need from two to six weeks to settle down. You are sure to be grateful when the period of confusing, helter-skelter eating and sleeping schedules ends. You are relieved that you are getting to know him and have a reasonable chance at predicting his eating and sleep needs.

NIGHT AND DAY

When the baby is born, he quite literally doesn't know night from day. You have the task of convincing him that there is a difference between the two.

As it happens, you'll teach the lesson without much thought: When your baby wakes for a night feeding, your response is naturally understated and very sleepy. His nursery is dark, except for a low, indirect light, like a nightlight. You say little or nothing and the room is otherwise very still. Your baby gets the not-so-subtle hint that nighttime is sleep time.

As your baby grows, his schedule will change. The number of feedings in each 24-hour period decreases. Depending on luck and the baby's needs, night feedings in the wee hours of the morning will taper off. You may well find that you can coax him to stretch sleep from midnight to dawn if you feed him just before you go to bed.

Sleep

Babies vary wildly in the amount of sleep they need and as he sleeps, so do you. This matter is so important that it is usually one of the first questions parents ask each other about their new babies. "How is he sleeping?" they ask. So-called "sleepers" are a blessing, while wakeful, active babies make parenting more difficult.

At one extreme are babies who sleep almost continually during the first few weeks, waking to be fed and to play a little while before drifting back to sleep. These babies clock eight hours during the night at a very early age. At the other extreme are the newborns who don't sleep more than ten to 12 hours in 24. (Parents of these wakeful babies have a special place in heaven reserved just for them!)

You cannot change your baby's sleep needs. Unless your baby is sick, he isn't having problems sleeping. *You* may be having trouble adapting to it. If your baby is especially wakeful, try to get in the habit of doing things for yourself as well as nurturing him. Unless he is in distress, you should be able to do a *few* things other than parenting him while he is awake.

You may find that it helps your baby to settle down to sleep if you designate one or two specific places where he is expected to sleep. Putting a baby down when he is ready in a certain setting helps the baby get sleep patterns organized. He learns to understand the signal from on high. The key here is to make sure he is ready. Only you can make that judgment.

TIP: Formulate a checklist of baby needs to go through before you put him down, to make sure he isn't hungry or bored.

As your baby reaches three months of age, he'll expand the periods when he is alert. He needs fewer naps, perhaps only two, lasting about two hours in the morning and two hours in the afternoon.

Unfinished Goals and Agenda

As we leave the first three months of your baby's life, we should remember the ground covered in Chapter 6. Every baby is a person in his own right, however tiny and helpless he may seem, with his own capacities for abilities and interests. What fascinates one baby will bore another.

As you read through the outline of goals for the first three months, try not to be overly worried about the gaps you see in development. You can encourage him to be more active or pay more attention to his hands and feet, *but you can't force him.*

If you have concerns, it may be best to take them to your pediatrician or family doctor. A consultation with an expert may help to relieve your anxiety and enable you to enjoy each part of babyhood as it deserves. Your baby will never pass this way again.

8

Expanding Horizons

The next six months as your baby learns to sit and crawl are full of daring explorations into space. As she learns, her world becomes larger and larger. Slowly but surely, and with lots of encouragement and help from you, she learns to strike out on her own.

Wobbly and uncertain, with many false starts and tumbles, she heeds the urgent drive to develop, which is universal among normal babies. Inexorably, she hones skills that buy her increasing independence and self-sufficiency, and help her explore and make sense of the world she lives in.

Before your baby masters the achievements of sitting independently and crawling, her investigations into the nature of the world are limited. In the first few months of life, what she sees is a function of where her parents put her. Confined to a spot on the floor on her tummy, or lying on her back in an infant seat, she sees only what happens to come into her field of vision.

This small world is all the baby needs in the early part of infancy. She has enough on her plate. She is busy adjusting to the sensations of her new environment, getting organized on a regular schedule of eating and sleeping, and learning to manage that disproportionate head.

After three months the baby has managed to turn and lift her head in any direction her neck allows and has raised her shoulders and upper chest off the mat. Her arms and legs alternate motions smoothly, but as yet she has little ability to govern what they do. The best she can do these days is take a swipe at an occasional target on the curtain-rod mobile you made for her in the last chapter.

Your baby will make enormous strides in development during the next six months. In months four through six, she will get to know her own body and begin to find out what she can do with it; in months seven through nine she will learn to sit alone, the midway point between lying down and standing up. She will also learn to creep and crawl, rehearsing for a debut on her feet, later on in Chapter 9.

Getting Control: Months Four, Five and Six

ROCK AND ROLL OVER

One of your baby's first goals is to take command of her body postures. Rather than crying when she is bored, calling for someone else to help her get a different view of things by turning her onto her tummy or back, she learns to roll over herself.

> Fresh from a nap, your baby lies on her stomach in her crib. She feels energized and begins doing baby pushups, lifting her head and chest off the ground. In a burst of enthusiasm she pushes harder with one arm than she does with the other. Boom! The world spins and over she goes. No one is more surprised than she is.

It may take her awhile to figure out what she did and repeat this feat of strength. What begins as an accident soon becomes an acrobatic delight. Your baby continues to practice until she can turn front to back as well.

A few babies take to rolling as their first means of getting from here to there. Some parents find they have to rescue their baby from all sorts of odd places as a result of these sideways somersaults.

There's no telling when your baby will make this breakthrough. Since the first time is always an accident, you must be careful never to leave your baby alone on a counter or other unguarded surface—even for a moment. She can make her move in a flash!

SITTING PRACTICE

As soon as your baby is able to hold her head up, she can sit with support in your lap for a short time. As her upper body muscles strengthen, she can increase the time. But she won't be able to sit unless you support her lower trunk and hips, which otherwise would sag.

Slowly, the lower torso muscles come into line. By the sixth month she needs only minimal lower back support and may even sit alone, leaning forward and using her arms as props. As your baby learns to sit alone, her back is wobbly and she waves her arms for balance.

She will make errors in balancing and topple over in any direction. To save her the bumps and hurts of her mistakes, you can surround her with rolled quilts or pillows to cushion her. You must never leave her alone while she is seated like this. If she were to fall on top of her arms and be unable to free them, she might suffocate.

SAFETY TIPS: Be ready for her before she learns to creep and crawl. Take a trip on your own hands and knees around your house. What can you see that might harm your baby? Remove whatever dangers you find. Clear low tables and lower shelves of items she would otherwise reach and shouldn't. Fit wall plugs with safety caps. Lock anything poisonous securely in a cabinet.

JUMPING FOR JOY

While some babies in this second quarter enjoy sitting peacefully in a lap, there are others who insist on making it their own personal trampoline. These babies delight in trying to pull themselves up (pulling on your hair, clothing, or whatever is handy) to stand. What they want to do is clear, but they need help getting up and support in standing. Once they are upright, they bend and straighten their legs exuberantly. These active babies will stand alone and walk sooner than quieter babies. (See Chapter 9 for more.)

MOVING OTHER MUSCLES

In the last chapter we left your three-month-old rhythmically moving her arms and legs, cycling them smoothly. Back then she was able to alternate their movements. Now when we see her in the next three months, she learns to move both arms and legs at the same time.

At six months old, she may start and stop them at will, and take a rest before intentionally resuming again. Exercise, for sure, but with a purpose. She learns a variety of tricks with her arms (see *Hand-Eye Coordination* below) and legs. She finds she can kick a dangling toy (remember the mobile you made earlier), get rid of her covers or make her stroller move (always put on the brake if you pause in an outing, and never leave the stroller unattended). Her infant legs and arms are learning to have an impact on the objects they can reach.

THE CREEP

At the outset, every baby has her own way of getting around. As we noted earlier, some babies are rollers. Now we look at the creepers. Using a war movie maneuver, babies inch along on their elbows, stomach and knees, moving imperceptibly forward, making slow progress across the floor. Left unattended, beds are hazards for these combat creepers: They creep over to the edge and topple over the side, discovering gravity can be unkind.

HAND-EYE COORDINATION

When we left her in Chapter 7, at three months of age, your baby was able to hold something in her grasp voluntarily. She was banging away at dangling toys, and rather inefficient in her aim. In the next three months your baby will learn to gauge and secure a target, first reaching with two hands, and then as skill increases, with only one hand. By six months she can rotate her wrist and explore a toy with a little more sophistication.

Her grasp is palmar, that is, she uses her fingers and palm. As yet her thumb has no role in grasping. She is unable to voluntarily let go of an object. If another object is offered, she will open her fingers automatically and drop whatever is in her hand. She will take a new object and put it immediately to her mouth, and then extend her arm to bang and shake it.

Personal Relationships

In the first three months of life your baby's social life is limited to a few smiles and a giggle or two. She is too busy getting her act together. The next three months see the debut of a social animal. Full of smiles and laughter, she will respond to talk with vocalizing. Other people have paramount importance to her; she is intent on getting attention from those close to her. She will smile or vocalize to interrupt a conversation that doesn't include her.

By six months she may be disturbed by strange adults. But she will react positively to unfamiliar children. Somehow she seems to recognize a child's kindred soul, and will try to engage his attention. She may even reach out and pat a child she has never seen before.

Cultural Habits

Your baby has settled in now. She recognizes ritual happenings, built into her schedule, like preparations for a meal or an outing after lunch (out comes the stroller, on goes the snowsuit, etc.) and greets the sight of accouterments with excitement. She gleefully anticipates what happens next.

Your baby may show interest in holding her own bottle and may begin using a cup, as a supplement to the bottle. As her physical and social life increases, a nursing baby will lose some or all of her interest in breast-feeding. A bottle-fed baby can turn in different directions as she drinks. A nursing baby is doomed to staring at her mother's chest. She may get bored.

In Chapter 7 we left our three-month-old needing one late-night snack, but otherwise sleeping through the night. In months four, five and six, your baby will drop her night feeding, and wake at dawn ready to eat and go.

Most babies sleep through the night by six months. (Some have been doing so for months, a few others won't do so for months to come.) Sometimes her sleep may be disrupted by nightmares. Cutting teeth commonly causes babies to sleep fitfully during the fourth, fifth and sixth months. You won't see the source of the problem until just before the first tooth breaks through, when you'll feel a small bump on her gum that pains her when you touch it.

Getting Control: Months Seven, Eight and Nine

SITTING ALONE

As your baby practices sitting by herself, she waves her arms about for balance or uses them as supporting tripods. While she is working to stay upright on her bottom, she can't use her arms to explore. But as she builds strength, skill and confidence, she won't need to use her arms to help her sit.

In the third quarter of her first year, the baby learns to sit with true independence. When her arms are free, she can explore the immediate area around her, twisting and turning her body, reaching for an object at will.

GETTING INTO POSITION

Once a baby learns to sit alone effectively, her interest in learning how to get into a sitting position intensifies. She has already been practicing for a few months now with help from you and her mother. In the third month the baby enjoys it when you pull her up. A little later she has the strength to hold on to your hands while *she pulls herself* to a sitting position.

Left alone, your baby likes to experiment. Right now she is trying to sit on her own:

> Your baby creeps over to the side of her crib. When she finds herself face to face with the crib bars, she reaches one arm up and grabs on. Then she reaches the other arm up as high as she can. Holding onto the bars, she hoists herself up, scrambles her legs up underneath and plops down into a seated position. She hangs onto the bars without the least idea of what to do next. She cries for help, and you, amazed at her new skill, pick her up and give her a hug.

As your baby learns to crawl, she will experiment until she learns how to get from her hands and knees to a seated upright position during months seven, eight and nine. (She will move her hands closer and closer to her body until she can rock back onto her bottom, and pull her legs out in front.)

LEARNING TO CRAWL

Active babies are usually not content with creeping. Inching across the floor is too slow for them. Though not yet ready for smooth hands-and-knees locomotion at six months of age, your baby may rise on her hands and knees, alternately or at the same time. Seesawing back and forth, she hurtles forward in a dramatic effort to get somewhere. Struggling valiantly, she achieves more forward progress than the creeping inchworm baby. She gets a bonus as well: She has a head start in learning to crawl.

Up and down, she practices baby pushups, feats of strength more difficult than those used to gain control of her head and upper body. These exercises build muscles that can support most of her own weight while she is on her hands and knees. A less active baby may spend a long time *thinking* about crawling while poised on her hands and knees. Without the drama of an active baby's efforts, you can almost see these babies discussing with themselves the best way to move.

OTHER WAYS TO GET AROUND

Not all babies crawl on hands and knees. Some never do. They are content to shuffle along on their bottoms, using hands and feet to guide them. This modus operandi is most efficient: Babies are ready to sit and play the instant they reach the toy they have their eye on.

Some babies do a sideways crab walk, with stiffened legs and arms. Good news for busy parents who don't have time to patch worn knees in overalls!

Once she is up on all fours, your baby's next challenge is to learn how to coordinate moving her limbs. She relies on trial and error as the method of learning. Her leg will move tentatively one way. No progress. Your baby may then try putting out her right arm and leg at the same time. Doing so, she leans too far in one direction and topples over. Finally, she figures out that she has to put forth her *opposite* arms and legs in order to crawl effectively.

Once she gets it together, life will never be the same, for her or for you.

HAND-EYE COORDINATION

Thumbs into action. During these next three months your baby's reach and grasp become quite sophisticated. Using thumb and forefinger as pincers, she learns to pick up a small pellet or string.

Now that her thumb helps her hold an object, she can manipulate it more readily.

She can reach out and grasp something without having to look first at her hand. More important perhaps, she can reach out and not grasp something, choosing to touch it or pat it instead. (Pets suddenly have an easier time of it now, though baby's hands are not necessarily gentle.) *Not* grasping something signals that your baby has learned a new kind of use for her hands. She knows to use them as tools for exploring. By the end of this three-month period, your baby may have gone beyond patting and be able to poke her forefinger into holes and crevices.

Personal Relationships

You remember your sociable little bundle during months four, five and six? In the next three months she learns the law of the squeaky wheel. She becomes more assertive and may shout for attention. She learns to use parents and others to get things for her. She will actively resist something she doesn't want to do and, if offered something she doesn't want, will push it away (a spoonful of spinach, perhaps?). She may stand up for her rights and fight to protect a disputed toy.

TIP: A struggle is much less likely to develop if you divert her by offering a substitute when taking something away (though if the something is dearly loved, this tactic may not work).

Balancing your baby's assertiveness is a budding sense of humor. She loves to perform for an audience and is eager to repeat an act that wins approval. Highly dependent on her mother, she follows her around the house (once she has learned to crawl effectively), and hates being separated from her.

Cultural Habits

Somewhere during these months, you may discover that a blanket, soft doll or stuffed animal will comfort your baby. This object, whatever it is, has a magical effect. With it under her arm she will settle down for sleep, either for a nap or bedtime. Soon the favored piece will be incorporated into the bedtime ritual or be brought along on a visit to the doctor. Tears and fears fade if this comfort, whatever it is, is close by.

BE PREPARED: Have a substitute on hand for when, not if, you lose it. But there's not much you can do if it is a one-of-a-kind treasure.

Your baby continues to learn to feed herself. She manages finger foods, like crackers or bits of banana, successfully. A cup provides all the liquid she needs, but it doesn't offer the comfort of a bottle or breast. She may even refuse to drink from a cup, if she thinks the bottle or breast might be withheld from her.

Sleep may continue to be a fretful time, with nightmares and teething being the major culprits. An average baby sleeps about 13 hours a day, with naps that vary from baby to baby.

The Road to Toddlerhood

Your baby has come a long way since we began this chapter. At the outset she was just able to raise her chest off the mattress. Now as we end the chapter she is bugging around the house after you, pulling on toilet paper rolls and disassembling stacks of kitchen pots and pans or the books by your bed. She can reshuffle piles of sorted laundry or organize your shoes her own special way. Wherever she goes, she'll turn things upside down.

As your baby pauses on the threshold of walking and beaming at light speed into toddlerhood, take a mental picture of her. Freeze the frame. Who is she? Take a moment to think back to what she was like as a newborn and in the first months. Paging through photos and her baby book will refresh your memory.

The contrast between then and now is astonishing, isn't it? You have been nurturing this baby from day to day, week to week. She grows a little every day, though you are probably too close to see it. Her progress snowballs, building skill upon skill, and all of a sudden your baby has vanished from your arms and a toddler appears—walking by your side.

9

Out on Two Limbs

As we open this chapter your baby gets around smoothly and quickly on the horizontal plane, in his own fashion: on his hands and knees, shuffling along on his bottom, or on straight arms and legs like a crab. By moving across the floor he learns about the space around him. Safely anchored on the ground, he expands the business of babyhood, exploring soft and hard, smooth and rough, heavy and light, as he goes.

Before your baby begins to pull himself upright, the world he can reach out and touch is still relatively flat, limited to forward and back, side to side. Moving from a sitting position to standing, your baby doubles the radius of his sphere of learning. He can reach all sorts of things he never could before. Now the top of a bookshelf and the top of the dining room table are fair game. You will have to analyze your home again and figure out how to cope with his expanded reach, then clear the area of dangers.

There are all kinds of problems your baby must solve once he gets up on his feet. First, he has to learn about "down" and how to get there. In addition, he has to work on independent means of getting up and down, as well as balance and taking steps. Learning to stand and walk takes months and months of concentrated effort. Let us go back to the beginning and trace the process that brings your baby up on his feet and into toddlerhood.

Getting Ready

As we saw in the last chapter, the seeds of standing alone are sown in the early months of "jumping" on adults' laps. With strong hands to hold him, your baby exercises to tone the leg muscles that must support him when he strikes out on his own.

At around seven months your baby continues his lap legwork, but refines the motion, alternating his legs, stepping in place, sometimes with awkward results. He may step on his own foot, pull out the one underneath, and place it back on top.

Up and down, up and down he goes, but without the urge to make any headway, seen so clearly in early creeping and crawling practice. Some babies never tire of these exercises; parents are exhausted long before their small charges are ready to quit. The more jumping and dancing he does, the sooner his legs will be able to support his upright body.

Parental patience is advised. Your hands are needed for support. He can't do it without you.

Pulling Up

This milestone has two prerequisites: Your baby must be able to take his full weight and he must have an opportunity to try his luck. He may pull himself up the same way he learned to pull up to a sitting position, by hauling himself up with the help of a crib bar.

> Waking from a nap one afternoon, your baby finds himself wedged in a corner of his crib. He talks to nearby stuffed animals for a while. Tiring of that, he reaches up as high as he can and grabs a crib bar. Pulling up, he is able to catch hold with a second hand and gather his legs under him. In a sit-kneel position he is able to walk his hands up the crib bars. As he does so, he can unfold his body upward. Once in a straight kneeling position, he raises one knee and puts one foot down on the mattress. In a final burst of strength he pulls up, bringing his other foot to rest on the mattress.
>
> Thunderstruck at his new view of the world, our brave young man peers over the crib railing. Soon his legs tire and he wants to stop standing, but hasn't a clue how to give his muscles a rest. So he cries out pitifully. Coming to the rescue, you are flabbergasted at your baby's new trick.

BABY STRENGTH TEST

As your baby gains strength, you can gauge his progress in taking his weight on his feet. With your hands holding his torso firmly under his armpits and supporting all his weight, hold him up in a standing position, feet on a hard surface like the floor. Ever so gradually, ease your grip until his legs begin to sag. At first his legs will sag like an accordion. By the end he will need your hands for balance only.

Cribs or playpens are stable and handy for your baby's stand-up practice. You are useful too, particularly if you are sitting on the floor accessible to your crawling baby. You feel tentative little hands pulling on your clothing, working their way up to shoulder level. Later on, he will use your pants leg as his ladder.

As your baby becomes adept at pulling up, he will go about testing furniture and other large objects to try out. He pushes on it or tries to shake it to see if it moves. After a little experimentation, unsteady pieces like a rocking chair or an open door will be readily discarded.

Your baby will learn to rely on sturdy objects like bureaus or desks, particularly because they have knobs or handles to grab onto. You must help him find out which objects around the house (i.e., the floor lamp, the ironing board, the stove) are unacceptable means to his goal.

Finding the Down Button

As we just noted, once they have gotten up, babies often don't know how to get down again. Perhaps because the first few times your baby pulls himself up are more or less accidents, his muscles don't remember the way back. In the beginning he scrambles over and pulls himself up. A minute or two later he tires or wants to go to a different spot and try again, and cries for help. You rescue him, then despair when he immediately repeats the exercise.

THE RIGHT SHOES, THE RIGHT SURFACES

Babies need to use their toes and feel the floor with their feet as they learn the techniques of standing and walking. Try to give your baby many opportunities to go barefoot as he is moving through the stages described in this chapter. Wearing socks without shoes is very slippery, unless they have a nonskid surface on the soles.

Once he is ready to try his skills outside, he will need shoes. To some extent, he will have to relearn his moves without "feeling" the floor. Shoes must fit perfectly and not allow too much room for growth. He should be able to move his toes freely. You should be able to press down with your finger just beyond his big toes. Too-large shoes increase the likelihood of tripping and exaggerate the way he takes a step. The soles should be sturdy but flexible, not hard and slick; the uppers a soft moccasin toe.

Before your baby gets too far on his feet, look around your house for danger zones. Take up all throw rugs without nonskid backings. Resist the urge to superwax hardwood or linoleum floors. If your floors are already slick, consider putting down nonskid rugs in high-traffic areas.

Take heart. Muscle memory comes with practice. He will learn either to bend his knees, let go and plop down, or he will inch his way back down the support structure the same way he came up. Don't try to force the issue by leaving him standing somewhere until he figures it out. If you do, most likely he will "solve" his problem by falling down, bruising his confidence.

After he knows how to pull up and get down smoothly, he will add small motor skills to his busy up-and-down life. He will learn to crawl over to the sofa with a small toy tight in his hand, and manage to pull himself up with one hand, clutching the toy in the other. Sofa and chair cushions are now his play area and you may find that toys collect there. He'll find other new places to play as well. For example, he may be delighted to discover a cabinet where he can pull up and bang a pot lid while you are busy in the kitchen. Sociable, if a little noisy.

THE PHYSICS OF STANDING

Judging from the number of adults seeking relief from back pain and the number of chiropractors and other professionals engaged in relieving their distress, human beings aren't really supposed to be upright. Our evolutionary ancestors began on all fours. Rising up on our two hind legs is a relatively recent adaptation of a horizontal skeletal structure.

Re-enacting the evolutionary process on a small scale, the skeletal frame and muscle structure of every new baby gradually adapt to life in the vertical plane. In the first year a baby is better suited to the horizontal plane. When a baby stands up and begins to walk, he may look a little funny. The toddling gait so familiar in a baby-almost-child is due to his physique:

Compared to an adult, a baby

- has a proportionately short neck,
- has a rounded rib cage,
- has relatively more bone than muscle,
- has long arms,
- is either bow-legged or knock-kneed.

As he grows over the next two years,

- his neck lengthens,
- his rib cage flattens,
- his muscles will thicken and grow faster than his bones.

When he finally takes that first step, he will be flat-footed, putting the entire sole of his foot directly on the floor. As yet there is no arch and no heel-toe walk. That comes later.

As he grows to be a child, he will become beautifully proportioned and walk on straightened legs.

Cruising

Within a couple of weeks of pulling up to stand, your baby learns to step sideways along the furniture he has been using to support him. He'll rise, facing the seat of a sofa or chair, and, without letting go, inch his hands along the edge. As his hands move along, one foot leads him into a sort of straddle. Not yet prepared to follow up with the other, and not knowing what else to do, he will likely sit down again.

As he learns to alternate his feet, he makes side steps, moving hand over hand along the support. Constant practice, known only to babies, golf pros and concert pianists, will get him up to speed. Soon he will have a favored cruising "course" from sofa to chair to coffee table, and so on, needing to hold on only for balance as he makes his rounds.

Holding Hands

When your baby is able to cruise with confidence, he will also be willing to take your hands and walk along. But beware. This is an awkward angle for your back because you must lean over and, at the same time, provide steadying support for him. If your back is temperamental, you are wise not to offer him the opportunity. He will walk in any event.

TIP: If you feel you must be careful of your back, but want to give him every opportunity to walk, you can share the duty with your mate, each taking one of his hands. Still a strain, but halved.

Investing in a walker is another alternative which places no strain on your back, but may create other problems. As his balance improves, he will need only one adult hand to get around. He will gradually take over more and more of the work, making it easier for you. One day he'll simply let go.

If you decide to use a walker, try not to invest in a new one. A walker can last through many babies. Friends' attics and thrift shops are good secondhand sources. Make sure it is very sturdy and stable. Clean it thoroughly, oil or spray the wheels with a lubricant—and off the baby goes!

In the absence of a rolling walker, your baby may find a make-shift one. As he cruises about, he may find a wood chair which moves as he pushes on it, enabling him to take a step. If he goes

THE WALKER DILEMMA

There is good news and bad news about walkers. First, the good news. It saves your back from strain and helps your baby learn to maneuver in an upright position. Walkers usually come with a play tray for toys as well as a flexible seat, so that your baby can sit and play, then stand up and bug around, as befits his mood and energy level. While your baby is in the walker, you know where he is and all the trouble he can't get into. It can become, if you will, a sort of moving playpen.

Now for the bad news. It can become a crutch that stifles experimentation. The walker does the work for him. A high-strung baby who exults in his instant, if false, success, may become wild, tearing from here to there, nonstop. As he bangs from sofa to table to chair, your furniture will take a beating.

And for all the trouble he doesn't get into, you may not necessarily get much peace. He can get stuck fairly easily, trying to get through a space that's too small, and squeal in frustration for you to rescue him. Or he may not be able to roll onto a rug from a hardwood floor with the same results. Walkers are downright dangerous in rooms with a ledge the baby can roll off or access to steps he can tumble down. You must use a walker only in rooms you can close off.

So much for the pros and cons. The answer may be a compromise. If there is an area in your home, relatively free of furniture and rugs, that you can close off, like the basement or kitchen, where you spend a certain part of each day, you may find a walker useful. Limit its use and the disadvantages are likely to fade.

with his discovery, he may push it all the way across the room, or at least until he gets stuck. If you wish, you can turn an old chair on its back and encourage him to push that one—and save your Chippendale for more conventional uses.

Letting Go

Up till now, your baby has been holding onto furniture, your hands or his walker in an effort to hold his body perpendicular to the earth, an amazing feat that adults may have trouble imagining. If you have ever been dizzy or woozy with a cold, then you have a clue, however inexact, to the task your baby is working on. He has come a long way since he started jumping and dancing on your lap. Now it is time to let go.

> Standing at his favorite chair one day, your baby is happily "reading" his favorite board book, turning the pages with one hand while resting the other on the cushion for balance. It looks almost as if the second hand is there out of habit, more than need. He spies a favorite toy he hasn't seen for awhile over on the sofa. He cruises over, stops, picks it up with both hands and examines it with interest, unaware that he has let go. A moment or two later, he suddenly realizes what he has done and immediately puts his hand back on the chair.

Again, accident is the instigator. Most babies are reluctant or frightened to let go, even if they are steady and sturdy on their feet. A few repeats of incidents like the one described above will convince him that nothing disastrous will happen when he stops holding on.

As soon as your baby finds he can stand alone, he naturally begins to incorporate the elevator skills of getting up and back down again without holding on. As of old, he moves from a sitting position to his knees and from there to his feet. But instead of reaching up for a handle or object to pull on, he learns to push off the floor with his hands. Ever so carefully, he straightens his body until he is fully upright. On the way back down, he folds up his body, bending over to put his hands back on the floor. They hold him steady while he puts his knee and bottom to the floor as well.

First Steps

Babies able to stand alone think about walking long before they take those first tentative steps. You'll see it in his face that he wants to move out, but is afraid to venture it. To help your baby break through his reluctance, you can hold your hands out as a safety net, urging him to take a few steps to your familiar, loving arms. He may take the cue, or he may decide to sit down and wait for another day.

If you are lucky, you will see your baby's first steps. It happens without warning. One day without any bidding, he may simply stagger from the cocktail table to the easy chair. And then return to crawling for days or even a week without trying out his new skill again. The experience of upward mobility may have upset him. Don't worry—he will try again another day.

Or he may relish his new mode of locomotion and once he starts, never stop. Though crawling is the business end of getting around for a while, tottering around engages most of his learning energy.

Be of Good Cheer

Your baby will fall down, often. This is the heartrending part of parenting. The job of learning to walk belongs to him, not to you. You can't prevent the bumps and lumps of experimentation, nor would it help him if you could. Your child must live his own life and fight his own battles. Flesh of your flesh, blood of your blood, he is quite separate from you. Your assignment, for now and always, is to encourage and cheer him as he presses on. Admire his courage. Your unending love and applause will fuel his fire to burn ever brighter.

10

Of Independent Means

During the second year of life your baby becomes a toddler, a stage between babyhood and childhood, analogous to the in-between adolescent child on her way to being an adult. An 11- or 12-year-old is often awkward. So, too, is your toddler, in a very different way, endearingly clumsy and inexpert. Both budding adult and nascent child take turns at exasperating and amusing their parents.

Growing up is painful. During the transition from baby to child, both you and your child suffer the aches of stretching. She'll become frustrated and angry at times. Venting her anger with a tantrum or another unpleasant display, like hitting or biting, the child will relieve her tension—on you and other members of the family.

While you must take steps to stop her hurting others (by immediately and resolutely saying No and removing her from the situation to her crib or other safe, designated spot where she can be alone for a few minutes), also try to understand the source of her frustration. Put yourself in her shoes. You may discover a way to help her over the hurdle that vexes her. At the least, you will salve your own anger and be able to cuddle and encourage her the next time.

This chapter looks at the physical milestones that your baby-almost-child may achieve from months 13 to 24. Logically, progress made during the second year will vary widely, depending on the base provided by first-year achievements. And remember what by now is quickly becoming an old saw in this book: Babies Are Different!

First-Year Portraits

LARGE MUSCLES

By the time the first candle flickers on their birthday cakes, most babies can maneuver on their feet in some way. Some will be walking a step or two. A few others may stand alone. Many more will be cruising around furniture with ease, able to let go momentarily. Others will still only be able to pull themselves up.

Your year-old should be able to sit alone. (If for some reason she is unable to do so, you had best consult your pediatrician.)

RIGHT AND LEFT

At a year your baby will prefer one hand over the other. In doing a more complicated skill, like opening a container, she will hold the object with one hand while her favored hand pulls on the lid. When she is feeding herself, watch which hand she uses.

As everyone who is left-handed knows, the world is right-handed. To a lefty, scissors are made backward, lecture hall seats have writing boards on the wrong side and bumping elbows at crowded dinner tables is a way of life. Indeed, there are now boutiques that carry merchandise tailored to the needs of lefties.

If you are right-handed, don't worry if she is a lefty. There is nothing wrong or inferior about it. *Do not* try to change her to a righty. All kinds of confusion and trouble lie ahead for children who have their preference for right and left altered. In earlier times it was not uncommon to switch a child. But experts agree now that a baby-toddler-child must find her own handedness.

Most likely she can sit with ease, turning in any direction to reach for a toy, fetch it and face forward with it safely in hand. She can get to a seated position either from her crawling hands and knees or from standing.

HAND-EYE COORDINATION

Her hands now use objects in important ways. Much of the information that she learns about her world comes to her through her fingertips. Consequently, once she has mastered the art of reach and grasp, she'll learn to push, pull, throw, fill and empty, albeit awkwardly. Touching, stroking and poking objects are tasks that fascinate her as well.

Personal Relationships

Your one-year-old is highly attached to her mother, and separation from her may cause havoc in the household. But that's not to say your young woman is clingy. She may well be content to play independently while Mommy is nearby, busy with other duties. Her desire to please is very strong. If either of you shows disapproval of something she's done, she may melt into tears.

While deeply in need of parental approval, your year-old child may seem uneven in her responses to the adults close to her. She seems to teeter on an invisible line, alternately choosing cooperation and self-assertive defiance. On the one hand, she understands simple requests and will obey a command. On the other, she will test her limits (and yours) by repeating acts that she knows are unacceptable. She will also take control of her eating and sleeping habits. She'll refuse to eat a meal or take a nap she sorely needs. There's nothing you can do to force her. This is her Declaration of Independence. Remember how far George III got?

Cultural Habits

TOILET TRAINING

It is doubtful that your year-old child is ready yet. She is only just beginning to learn the signal of her need to void. Until she understands fully what that means, she can't learn to use the toilet or signal her needs to you.

Your baby may have a regular pattern that runs like a clock and you may be tempted to "catch" her. Don't. You'll find that she will hate being suddenly whisked away from play or when waking from a nap, being undressed and put on the pot. She doesn't care yet that she's wet or dirty. She gets nothing from the experience. She'd much rather either continue playing or be cuddled as she wakes up. You're likely to find that even though she doesn't protest at first, soon she'll begin to fight it.

EATING AND SLEEPING

Your year-old baby eats three meals a day, usually by her own hand. The sizes of her meals vary. As noted above, she may limit a particular meal to three peas and two bites of a roll. (She is perfectly content, though you won't be.)

Sleeping is often difficult these days. At the end of a day your baby is wound up and unwilling or unable to stop. Now that she is up on her feet and moving about, she is discovering and learning at an amazing pace. Her newfound skills open up vast new worlds to conquer. Novelty and the effort to assimilate it is exciting, but exhausting. At bedtime she may be unable to quiet herself, particularly if others in the household are still up and moving.

Year-olds find their own way of settling down, often choosing a rhythmic movement. Some babies rock on their hands and knees, others roll or bang their heads. More active babies will rock and roll their crib across the room, a true test of a manufacturer's product. Not all babies are so violent. Quieter babies may find their thumb or fingers to help them through the night.

Nearly a Year and a Half

WALKING

During this six-month period, your toddler moves out in earnest on her feet. First tentative steps turn into a rapid running walk. This gait may strike fear in your heart. You doubt your child's ability to stop or turn to avoid collisions. Even more troublesome is the realization that, like lightning, your toddler can careen from the sidewalk into the street and oncoming traffic.

By 18 months your toddler has much more assurance when she walks. She has learned how to stop without falling and she rarely falls in transit. She has become sufficiently sophisticated in her movements that she can walk sideways while pulling a toy.

CLIMBING

Some babies are climbers. This is not news to parents who early on must cope with their upwardly mobile offspring. All children learn to climb, but some are fanatics about it. Whether it comes early or late in your child's development, climbing has a high potential for disaster.

Your child may begin climbing by escaping out of her crib:

Your toddler wakens with the birds one morning, and pulls herself up on her feet. Finding herself standing next to a favorite stuffed bear, she steps on its head and throws her other leg up to catch the top crib rail. She latches her foot on it and pulls her other leg up, too. Precariously balanced on the crib rail, she doesn't know what to do next. Teetering, she finally falls. The ground surges up and hits her with a flash of pain. Her panicked wails jar you from sleep, and you rush to rescue and console her.

Removing the large animals from a crib and lowering the crib mattress will delay but not end the efforts of a climber. Resolute in her goal, she presses on. Before long, she will be climbing furniture, jungle gyms, stairs and anything else that's handy. Each frontier your toddler scales presents the same problem— how to get down safely.

At best, when she is stuck she will stop and call for help. At worst, she will lose her balance or try to get down alone—and fall. Under the motto of "If you can't beat 'em, join 'em," you'll do well to teach her how to get down from whatever spot she can get into. Physically moving each leg through the motions of down may help her learn. She may resist your help, preferring to do it alone. In either case, you must be there to catch her!

Some things, like stoves and bookshelves, make dangerous ladders. It is your job to either remove the piece or otherwise prevent her from climbing on it. In addition, you may want to consider switching her from a crib into a bed.

Squatting, Stooping and Sitting in Chairs

As your toddler becomes more at home on her feet, she will revise her methods of playing on the floor. In her first year she mastered the art of sitting upright on her bottom. Now she is no longer content to do so. She finds squatting or stooping more useful and efficient as she moves through her day. Using these skills she can walk over to an item of interest, stop and either stoop over to pick it up or fold up her body into a squat to examine or maneuver it.

SQUATTING AND STOOPING

Neither squatting or stooping come easily. Both require a virtuoso display of balance. She is likely to begin stooping while holding on, getting used to feeling her torso bend over and down, while she grips the ground with her feet as well. She learns to pick up an item with one hand and then return to standing. Up and down she practices, until she can let go.

Squatting is learned in much the same way. Holding an adult's hand or the drawer pull of a bureau, she will carefully lower herself down onto her haunches. When her body is safely folded and centered over her feet, she then lets go to build a tower of blocks, or examine and perhaps squash a hapless bug crawling across her path.

SITTING IN A CHAIR

While stooping and squatting are practical techniques your toddler uses to bend down to ground level, sitting down in a chair is her effort to gain entrance to the grown-up world. Her first attempts at getting into a chair and sitting down are clumsy, likely to be off center, requiring her to catch herself and shift over onto the seat.

Learning to back up to a chair and sitting down directly require your toddler to have a sophisticated awareness of her body in space. She must be able to judge distances and control her body to reach her goal. You will see her look over her shoulder as she inches backwards toward the chair. Soon she'll learn to plop down into a child-sized chair with reasonable accuracy. (Adult-sized chairs require a toddler to climb up, then turn around and pull her feet out in front.)

HAND-EYE COORDINATION

Once your toddler is walking successfully, she'll be better able to concentrate on expanding her dexterity in handling the objects she touches. She learns to react to a toy in many ways: She may twist or turn a knob, pull off a lid and dump out its contents, as well as push and poke a "busy box."

Successful handling of a toy is a symphony of hand-eye coordination and arm control. Building a small tower of two blocks is a good example of technique. Many complicated maneuvers are required to complete this relatively simple task.

Pretend that you are a novice construction backhoe driver sitting in the cab looking at levers which control the up, down and side movements, as well as the opening and shutting of the pincer jaws. As your first test, your boss tells you to pick up one box and place it on top of another. You see what to do, but achieving your goal is something else again.

You find you must separate the functions of each lever and practice each in turn, learning when and how to start and stop each action in time to reach your goal. When you have worked your way across the instrument panel, having mastered each aspect of it, you are ready to take on all functions at once, however awkwardly and poorly. Like babies and toddlers, you learn that practice makes perfect. Once you have stacked those boxes, your boss immediately comes up with a different, more difficult task for you. And so it goes.

Personal Relationships

The initial negativism and self-assertion we see at a year intensify during the next six months. Your toddler's drive for independence is fierce. "No!" may be her first word. In addition, she will say No by using imaginative body language and shrieks, leaving no doubt where she stands on a particular issue, like getting dressed or holding onto a toy.

But for all her efforts at independence, she is anxious to be close to you and is happiest when you are nearby. Your toddler is selfish and demands attention. Her social life is still limited. She takes, others give. But a glimmer of light is on the horizon as you discover that she is beginning to do what she is told.

Cultural Habits

TOILET TRAINING

By 18 months some toddlers are ready for toilet training. Once your child connects the feeling of pressure with the soiled diaper that results, she'll be able to learn to alert her parents for help. If she finds being soiled unpleasant, she'll be motivated to do so. Until then, she will be perhaps the only member of the household who is *not* aware of the event, as babies and toddlers commonly turn beet red and grunt while in the act.

It seems logical enough: Awareness plus discomfort equals success. Wrong. Toilet training is a tricky business between parent and toddler.

> While clearing away the breakfast things, your wife is waiting for your toddler to tell her that she is preparing to move her bowels as she often does after breakfast. Heartened by recent toileting successes, your wife sneaks a peek at her every once in awhile. Nothing happens, so they go out for an errand.
>
> The minute they are in the car and pulling out of the driveway, your toddler immediately moves her bowels. Your wife checks for diarrhea. Everything is normal. She strongly suspects that the child was simply waiting to leave the house, withholding the movement from the toilet and from her.

When toddlers become aware of bodily functions, they also realize that they own them. At the same time, they get a message that parents are anxious to stop the increasingly odious and expensive task of diapering. Toddlers realize that they are in control with a powerful weapon in their arsenal. The stage is set for a battle of wills, if not full-scale war.

TAKE IT GENTLY: Try to defuse the situation. Don't treat it as success or failure. Don't turn it into a gift she can either give or take away. Emphasize to her that being dry and clean is for *her* comfort.

Two Years Old

SITTING

Your two-year-old learns to seat herself at a small table for an imaginary tea with dolls or plain, real-life juice and crackers.

HAND-EYE COORDINATION

Skills in handling toys continue to improve. Your two-year-old may tackle a variety of complicated tasks, like stringing or snapping beads together, fitting pegs into holes or pushing shapes into a form board. These days the tower she can build may be as high as five stories.

RUN, DON'T WALK

Your toddler at two has refined walking to a fairly high level. She has learned to walk around obstacles, so that she doesn't bump into things. She can look over her shoulder while pulling a toy. She can walk backwards a few paces or approximate walking on a straight line. She takes stairs up and down with both feet on each step while holding onto the railing.

However, most toddlers this age would much rather run than walk. And she runs wherever she goes without being able to stop or turn, a problem similar to her early walking days, and equally dangerous.

In addition to running, your two-year-old loves to dance, jump, throw and climb. Always moving, exhausting you long before she tires, she is a good approximation of a perpetual motion machine.

Personal Relationships

Your two-year-old's ability to communicate gives a big boost to her social skills. Using words and gestures, she can make her interests, wants and needs clear to her family. She can relate an experience and express her feelings quite intelligibly.

While your toddler learns to make herself understood, she also learns to judge what others expect of her. Your two-year-old begins to form a sense of what is and what is not acceptable behavior. As you communicate with her and she understands what you expect of her, she will be more organized and less volatile in her everyday behavior.

Cultural Habits

BLADDER TOILET TRAINING

Some two-year-olds are ready for daytime bladder toilet training. Urinary training is usually more difficult than bowel training. The child's bladder is small and several trips to the toilet are required each day. You will also find it harder to identify your toddler's need to urinate.

As with the bowel toilet training, this can easily become a battleground, too. Your toddler has to *want* to be dry before any success is possible. And even if she wants to be dry, she may decide that she doesn't want to sit on the toilet or potty. She may stay dry in her diaper for a long stretch of time, urinate and then cry to be changed.

Just as toddlers resist being hurried in other aspects of their daily lives, they may also balk at being hustled off to the toilet several times a day. Your child quite naturally wants to take her own time about it. There are other reasons she may refuse to be toileted: fear of falling down the huge hole of the toilet, or the instability of sitting some place other than the floor. She may wish to withhold the "gift" that has suddenly become so important to you.

The issue of control between parent and child is explosive, a potential source of rancor throughout the second year at mealtimes as well as bedtime. You can avoid battling in the bathroom if you approach toilet training as a measure of comfort for your toddler, rather than as an achievement.

Your Grown-Up Baby

The second birthday is a time to stop and take stock. Your baby has sandwiched a lot of growing up into 24 months. She has managed astonishing feats of balance, strength and coordination. Little by little, she has graduated from lying down to standing up, from inching forward on her elbows to running full tilt. In the beginning she was a bundle of reflex actions. Now she can build a small tower with blocks. Looking back over the last two years, her accomplishments are huge.

The brisk pace of her development sparks pride in your chest. It also should remind you that your child has not been here very long. Most likely she looks more grown-up than she really is. Parents often fall into the trap of expecting too much from a baby who has learned the skills of a toddler.

A child of two is just beginning to sort out the complicated world around her. To her every day is an extraordinary experience. A walk around the block is a giant adventure, an invitation to try out new skills. It will be years before everyday events shrink to normal proportions.

Don't rush. Give her time to learn. Comfort and encourage her when she falters. She deserves it.

PART III

RAISING A HAPPY BABY

Raising a happy child does *not* mean shielding your baby from every bump in life. Your job as a father is not to overprotect him, but to prepare him for battle. You must introduce him to the vagaries of the world gradually and carefully.

You know your baby is remarkable. He has an innocence and grace which separates him from everyone else. His zeal to conquer his world, to comprehend and remember huge volumes of information and to master complicated motor skills is impressive. You marvel at his tenacious dedication to this play/work assignment.

But he is a person, not a saint. Failure and frustration are his constant companions and ill humor on occcasion isn't surprising. Indeed, it should be expected. Allow your baby the right to have moods, whether happy, sad or downright mad.

Just as you must allow for his moods and have respect for him as he grows up, you must give yourself some room, too. You need time alone and time with your wife. Both of you must look realistically at who you are and what you can give to your child. As parents you can't be everywhere and do everything, nor should you try to.

Every child is different. Your child may respond well to one approach, but resist another. What works for a neighbor's child may not help your child's situation in the least. The best way to ensure having a (mostly) happy baby and be reasonably content yourself is to gather some general rules for effective parenting and to make them work for *you.*

In these pages we suggest some ways to help your child grow from a completely helpless innocent to a walking, talking individual with opinions and a mind of his own. Equally important, we will help you understand how to cope with the miraculous transition of your baby into a toddler. These guidelines are not pie-in-the-sky platitudes. Our hope is that you will find them to be realistic, reliable tools which can make your life easier and your child's life happier.

11

On Becoming a Person

If you were to summarize your baby as a newborn, you might say: "Eager beaver with tremendous potential but no work experience, available for on-the-job training." And true to form, she wastes no time in starting to explore her environment and getting to know the people around her. In the short span of 12 months she firmly establishes her individual personality within the constellation of your family. By her first birthday it will be hard to remember what life was like without her.

The first year of your baby's life is a special time. As she swings from one month to the next, you will naturally savor every mannerism she adopts and each tiny achievement she makes. In the same breath, however, you may also worry about how you should raise her and how well you are doing as parents. Here we discuss these concerns and suggest some ways of handling the problems that are likely to arise in the first year.

Sorting Things Out

The transformation your baby undergoes during her first year is quite remarkable. At birth she emerges from the womb armed only with some useful reflexes and a good pair of lungs. Now that she is on her own, she must learn to breathe and eat. She is a stranger in a strange land—nothing she sees is familiar. Undaunted by the hugeness of her ignorance and completely unaware of her vulnerability, she fits bits and pieces of the world together and establishes a comfortable niche therein. So successful is she that by the end of her first year she has become a formidable explorer, playmate and companion.

SETTLING IN

Your newborn baby will need six to eight weeks to settle into her life. Until she establishes a pattern of eating and sleeping, your days and nights with her will be very unpredictable. You often won't know for sure what your baby wants or when she'll want it.

This uncertain period of adjustment can be quite distressing, even overwhelming to new parents. Take some comfort from knowing that this is an unavoidable and necessary time of transition. The fact that these first weeks are so erratic is not your fault or the baby's—it is nature's way of introducing you to each other. When your baby finally settles down, she will establish a routine and you will feel more confident in your ability to meet her needs.

These weeks can be exhausting and draining, but they don't

SOME HINTS TO MAKE YOUR LIFE EASIER

- Always use the same routine to put her to bed. Put her in the same place every night.
- Help her learn that nighttime is sleep time by making night feedings as low-key as possible. Keep the lights dim when you feed and change her. Say very little to her and return her immediately to her crib.
- Babies are usually hungry when they wake in the morning, so feed her first thing and if she fusses a few hours later, try feeding her again.
- Develop a routine when you feed her to help her identify a pattern in her life.

have to be. It is important to conserve your strength and get sleep whenever you can. Toward that end you should:

1. Sleep when your baby sleeps.
2. Eliminate all but the essential chores around the house.
3. Recharge your batteries by getting out of the house every day—with or without your baby in tow. Rejoin the human race, even if only for a short while.

SATISFYING HER NEEDS

Crying is the only way your baby can tell you she needs something. Using the time-tested method of trial and error, you'll respond to her call and endeavor to satisfy her needs. You'll develop a mental list of possible needs or problems to check every time she cries. While *hunger* and *tiredness* should be at the top of your list, don't forget to consider the following:

- Indigestion or other physical discomfort
- Illness (Does she have a fever or other symptoms?)
- Boredom (Has she been in one place too long?)
- Overstimulation (Does she dislike being undressed or having a bath? Perhaps too much is going on.)
- A desire to be cuddled (Your baby can feel lost and need the warmth and reassurance of familiar arms.)
- General crankiness (A grab bag of causes: parental tension and anger or nervousness, as well as her own frustration at her inability to communicate or accomplish a goal.)

JITTERY BABIES

All babies need special handling, especially at first. Newborns come equipped with the Moro, or startle reflex which can be triggered by sudden bright lights and noise and jerky, inexpert handling. Sometimes even the loudness of her own cry can startle your baby and start a chain reaction of distress. (Placing your hand gently but firmly on her chest or back will interrupt the sequence and calm her down.) Until the reflex fades, babies need a low level of stimulation and a gentle touch.

Some babies are more sensitive to stimuli than others. Their sensitivity remains long after the startle reflex fades. They object

CRYING TIMES

Every baby is different and some babies cry more than others. A few are truly miserable.

Colic

A common cause of misery is colic. Though no one really understands what it is, theories and remedies abound. Swallowed air from prolonged crying or overfeeding and indigestion have been suggested as sources of these babies' discontent. If your baby is colicky, you'll naturally try anything you can to get her to feel better. What may help:

- Walking with her upright over your shoulder
- Laying her face down on your knees
- A ride in the car
- Feeding her no more than 32 ounces of formula per day
- Offering a pacifier for extra comfort
- Letting her ride on your chest in a cloth front carrier as you move about.

End-of-the-Day Blues

Most young babies get cranky at the dinner hour. This swelling of unhappiness coincides with the low point of both parents' energy and strength. The end of the day is not necessarily the end of the chores around the house, and the journey home from work is frequently both long and tiring. What can you do?

Basically, you have two alternatives:

1. One of you can put the baby in a front carrier and go ahead with straightening the house and making dinner,

or

2. You can turn your full attention to your baby and ignore the "to do" list. Straightening the house at this hour may not be essential, nor does dinner have to be complicated. If neither of you feels like cooking, order in from Sal's Pizzeria.

if they are handled carelessly and react strongly even to normal stimulation. Babies like these require extra care because regular aspects of their daily routine, such as being undressed or having a bath, may be upsetting.

If your baby is hypersensitive to stimulation, you can:

- Give her a sponge bath occasionally instead of a full bath.
- Plan ahead so that you don't have to hurry somewhere with her in your arms.
- Swaddle her in a receiving blanket or crib blanket when she sleeps.
- When you are going to lift her up, approach her from the front, never from behind.
- Keep surprises to a minimum and play with her gently.

Growing to Love

When your baby is born, you and she are relative strangers. While you eagerly examine every inch of her body, she gazes back at you with interest. Her vision is acute at about eight inches and she sees you clearly whenever you hold her in your arms.

It is no accident that your newborn baby needs several small meals each day: The small portions suit her small digestive system, while the frequency of these feedings allows you ample opportunities to get to know—and love—each another. As you feed her, she engages your attention by making eye contact. For the sake of variety she may reach up and pat your chest.

Parents are constant companions and she learns at a very young age that you are essential to her well-being. When she trumpets her dependence by calling for you, you'll know that she has made the connection between love and need.

THE FIRST SMILE

As a newborn your baby cannot relate to you. She simply cries and then quiets when her problem is being solved. Except in the abstract, parenting in the first eight weeks can be a thankless task. You care for your helpless baby without receiving any acknowledgment from her other than the blessed peace and quiet that ensue when her needs are being gratified.

Then comes the first time she looks up and flashes a big toothless smile. The two of you have made contact. Your parental booster rockets fire and life is forever changed. That first smile tells you that she recognizes you as a person. Though she doesn't yet know you are separate from her, she associates you with comfort and pleasure. It won't be long before she stops crying when she sees you—even *before* you tend to her needs. Unfortunately, the opposite becomes true as well. She will reach the stage when she'll start crying when you leave her, too!

SEPARATION

Your young baby has a primitive understanding of objects. In the first six months she will watch objects that come into her view and then lose interest in them when they disappear from view. For her they no longer exist and she will turn her attention to something else. As she develops skills, she'll become more involved with a particular object, but once it is explored thoroughly or if it, too, disappears from sight, she will move on to the next toy.

Her parents, however, are objects of extreme importance to her and she is always keenly interested in your whereabouts. The attachment between you is a double-edged sword: While you are pleased that you are so successful at meeting her needs, you might be just as happy if she could do without you—just for a little while.

She has trouble being away from you. You are her link to her inner self and the world. Not only do you supply all her needs, you give her the sense of identity and security she needs. You interpret the world that is so confusing to her. It really should come as no surprise that she protests strenuously when you leave her from the time she is about eight months to 15 months old. (In some cases separation problems may last well into the third year.)

Babies don't have any sense of future and they have very little memory of the past. So we can't say that your baby actually misses you and yearns for the time when you will return. But she feels your absence acutely and is limited in the ways she can cope

GUIDELINES FOR SAYING GOODBYE

- Develop a routine that she can recognize. Say the same simple words to her each time. Don't make an elaborate or overly emotional display when you leave. Kiss and hug her, say your piece and leave. Don't go back for another kiss or make her wave Bye-bye. (If you make her wave, you are forcing her to say she accepts the fact you are leaving, even if she doesn't.)
- If you are leaving for just a few minutes, say so. She'll learn to remember your words and associate them with short-term absence. Do what you can to help her understand the difference between long and short separations.
- *Never* sneak out while she isn't looking. This is easier for you in the short term, but in the long run she'll become much more anxious about your being close by.
- Allow some time before you must leave to get her settled with the person who is going to take care of her. Give a treat or suggest a game to play after you leave.
- Always use the same caregivers. It is easier for her to calm down in the arms of someone she knows. Strangers are often anathema to babies.
- If your child is a toddler, tell her where you are going and what you'll be doing while you're away. Tell her some of the fun things she'll be doing, too.
- *Always be upbeat.* If you show her your feelings, she won't fare any better and she may very well feel worse than ever about your leaving.

with it. She can't count the minutes or watch the clock as older children can. She can't understand the concept of "being back by noon"—nor, for that matter, can she rely on your return at all.

SEPARATION AND FEELING GUILTY

Not every baby handles separation the same way. Your baby may be devastated when you leave, or she may protest at first and then settle down soon after you depart. How strongly she reacts depends on her personality and how you handle your departure from her.

Your baby needs you to be calm and matter-of-fact when you are leaving her. If you are overly emotional at leave-taking, she'll be even more upset than she would be otherwise. You are signaling her that something important—and terrible—is happening to her.

Prolonged emotional goodbye scenes often spring from feelings of parental guilt. It *is* hard to leave your child if you know or fear that she'll be miserable while you're gone. One of the major tasks you face as a parent is coping with the feeling that you have failed your child. To combat these guilty feelings, take a look at your parental role.

BE REALISTIC: You can't always be with your child. Nor should you be. Both of you need to get away from your baby to recharge your batteries either occasionally or on a regular basis. Indeed, you may not have a choice if your family needs two salaries to make ends meet. Whatever your situation is, rest assured that your child will learn to cope with it.

Finding Good Child Care

In general there are three types of care: structured day-care centers for a large number of children, family care, which offers more informal care for a small group of children in a private home, and a caregiver who comes to your home.

If your child is very young, you should probably consider either a family care environment or hiring a one-on-one caregiver for your child. She is likely to fare better in a cozier, flexible setting than she would in a highly structured day-care center. It is easier for her to adjust to a home environment and she will be less likely to feel lost there.

What's more, you may have some trouble finding a place for her in a large day-care center. Because the ratio of adults to babies is low, usually about one to three, and therefore more costly, such centers either limit the number of babies and under-twos they can accept or often refuse to take them at all.

AN IN-HOME BABYSITTER

Word of mouth, help wanted advertisements and employment agencies are the three main ways of finding a babysitter. Rather than choosing one method over the others, you'll be better off picking two or even trying all three. You won't be able to tell beforehand which will be the most useful to your search.

When you start gathering names, your next step is to conduct preliminary telephone interviews. Ask them (1) why they want a job caring for your child, (2) what they are doing now, (3) why they are leaving (or left) their last job, (4) their salary and job requirements, (5) if they have references you can check. If you are satisfied with the answers you get, you can then proceed to outline the job requirements and the salary you are paying.

Schedule a personal interview with those who pass the telephone interview test. Make sure your child is present so you can see how they react to each other. Watch how the prospective sitter engages your child. If she is confident and approaches your child in an appropriate way, you can then discuss theories of discipline and child rearing. If you are suitably impressed with a candidate, obtain the references and check them thoroughly.

Whether you choose family care or an individual babysitter will depend upon what is available in your area and what you can afford. Whether the caregiver comes to your home or runs the service in her own home, you'll need to make sure that both her philosophy of child rearing and her manner with your child are compatible with your own. (NOTE: While more men are being hired as nannies and babysitters these days, it is still overwhelmingly a female occupation.) The best way to find good, consistent child care is to visit the home and interview the caregivers.

When you have hired a person who seems to meet your criteria, and before your wife or you start the new job, allow at least a week for your child and new caregiver to get acquainted. In the beginning of the transition week leave her for a short period, and gradually extend your absence until it equals the time you will be gone for work. Because this is the perfect time to fine-tune her care, watch how the sitter is coping and how your child is reacting. When you make suggestions about your child's care, be as tactful as you can, but be sure your wishes are clearly understood.

Continue to monitor your child's care as long as she is in the caregiver's hands. Drop in unexpectedly once in awhile to make sure the verbal reports at the end of the day match what actually happens. If they don't, you may have to change caregivers.

FAMILY CARE HOMES

Word of mouth and child care referral services, run by municipalities or nonprofit organizations, are the best ways to find family homes in your area. Many homes are licensed, others are not. You should not assume that a license automatically means that the home is appropriate for your child, or that homes without a license are not satisfactory. Some states don't license family homes; others require that homes meet the standards used for larger day-care centers, which can be inappropriate and unrealistic for small child care enterprises.

Visiting family homes and watching the caregiver in action will help you decide which environment is best suited to your child. Observe her manner with the children and the types of activities she encourages. Are the children playing happily? How are crises handled? Other key elements to watch for: appropriate and accessible play equipment and toys, safety, overall cleanliness and nutritional meals and snacks.

When you are satisfied with the environment in a family care home, make an appointment to interview the caregiver. Set a time when she can give you her full attention and won't be diverted by the needs of her charges. In talking with her, you can ascertain her knowledge of child development and her approach to child rearing and discipline. In lieu of checking references as you would with a one-on-one sitter, talk with other parents of children in her care.

Sleeping and Eating

Your baby may be wakeful or sleepy, a picky or ravenous eater, or somewhere in between. The kind of baby she is depends on her metabolism, her level of activity, her genetic makeup and her personality. In general, babies who eat well or who readily fall asleep and sleep regular hours don't cause much parental concern. Often parents don't worry even when their good little eaters become obese, a condition that pediatricians agree is not healthy for children.

But what about the ones who from birth sleep very little or are choosy about what they eat? Even though wakeful or picky babies are just as likely to be normal, these are the babies that pediatricians hear complaints about. They cause an uproar because they exhaust their parents. If left on their own to devise their schedules and preferences, most of these babies would be perfectly content.

Some parents are determined to intervene and change schedules and mealtimes to suit themselves, not their babies. When that happens, a fight ensues and potentially happy babies (and their parents) become quite the reverse.

THE CASE OF THE WAKEFUL BABY

A wakeful baby is often more active than her peers and exhausts her parents long before she tires. If your baby fits this description, you probably feel that you'll never be rested again. Your life outside parenting has all but vanished. Though she doesn't need to change her lifestyle (indeed she would protest any regimen you try to impose), you definitely need a break.

Don't try to change her. As time goes by, she will become less demanding (though no less wakeful) and more competent at taking care of herself. While you are waiting for her to grow up, here are three suggestions to shore up your sanity:

1. Consider using a playpen. Introduce her to it when she is about two months old. Don't put her there all the time—just when you want a little peace.

2. Hire either household help or a regular babysitter—or both, if possible.

3. Learn to double up. You can start dinner or listen to a book on tape while watching her play. Invite a friend to come by for a visit. Use a little ingenuity to increase your productivity and your *satisfaction* with life in the fast lane.

THE CASE OF THE PICKY EATER

If your baby is finicky about what she eats, you may be worried that she'll become undernourished. If her pediatrician reassures you that she is gaining weight and growing normally, your immediate concerns are diminished. But though you are relieved, you still must cope with a picky eater every day.

Her demands can vary, but they are seldom negotiable. Here are a few of the possibilities:

1. She may strictly prefer nursing and refuse a relief bottle (some babies are known to wait *hours* for Mom to return).
2. She may require frequent small feedings rather than larger meals at longer intervals (other babies learn to stretch the time between feedings and whittle the number of feedings down to about five a day).
3. She may refuse baby food completely for weeks and demand her bottle or breast instead.

NOTE: Breast milk or formula should be her primary source of nutrition until her first birthday, and until then, solid foods are supplemental. During her second year, milk or other milk products should remain an important part of her diet.

What to do? If your baby seems to feel strongly on an issue, let her have her way, as long as the pediatrician agrees. Make well-baby visits to her doctor to ensure that she is, in her own fashion, making progress. If she refuses to be weaned or to eat baby food, don't force the issue. Wait awhile and then try again. When she is ready, she will unlock her jaws and accept the baby food you offer, as well as give up her beloved bottle or breast—though most likely not at the same time.

Comforting Your Baby

Your baby, along with every other baby ever born, needs comfort and comforting. Cuddling is as important to her as eating and sleeping. Without it she won't develop properly or be a happy baby.

Don't be reluctant to pick her up often because you fear she may become spoiled. Give her all the hands-on love and play time you can and comfort her when she is out of sorts. A baby less than a year old cries because she needs something (see *Satisfying Her Needs* checklist on page 128), not because she is trying to manipulate you. Soothing your baby when she is crying will not alter her personality. What will cause problems is *not* trying to make her feel better.

In addition to physical closeness with you, your baby needs other comforters. She will experiment and finally settle on one or two things that work for her. Comfort measures often center around sucking: She may choose her fingers, her thumb, or accept a pacifier to satisfy her needs. Sometimes repetitive motion like rocking and head banging (be sure to pad the sides of her crib well), or favorite items like a blanket or toy will also help her feel better.

These help her to calm down after overstimulation, go to sleep after a busy day, to be separate from you, and much more. Your baby learns while on the move. She constantly practices new accomplishments and may find it difficult to stop. When she does, she needs the extra help that her chosen comforter provides.

TIP 1: Prolonged thumb and finger sucking causes some real dental concerns. It can ultimately alter the structure of your child's mouth and you must decide when she should stop her habit. As a general rule, thumb and finger sucking during the first year is considered all right. Many children suck their thumb or finger during their second year, too, without any adverse effects.

TIP 2: A pacifier is not usually a cause of dental problems, but it can be overused. Don't offer a pacifier simply to stop your child's protests regardless of their origins, or inhibit her natural self-expression.

Meeting Needs

During your baby's first year most of the keys to her happiness lie in your meeting her needs appropriately. She requires you to understand, appreciate and nurture her budding personality. If you know who your baby is and what she is trying to do, and you offer her a chance to do it in a secure and loving environment, then she will be ready to face the challenges of toddlerhood ahead.

While you are busy meeting your baby's needs, don't forget to think of your own needs and those of your mate. Parenting is hard work and your efforts deserve a reward—many rewards. To that end, make a list of morale boosters—both large and small—that will lift your spirits and keep your marriage on track. Try an evening out or a couch potato special: Chinese take-out for two with a sexy movie on the box.

12

Making Life Easier

"When he's happy, you're happy."
—ANONYMOUS

We have said that parenting is hard work; indeed, it's a 24-hour, seven-day-a-week job. Both parents and child benefit if the daily routine is as pleasant and trouble-free as possible. To achieve this you will want to eliminate all the unnecessary hassles and hazards and establish a structure to your baby's day that is compatible with his personality, stage of maturation and energy level. You must understand his capabilities and his limitations and plan your lives accordingly. If you don't, he'll have to adapt to adult ways and become frazzled and exhausted with the effort—hardly the picture of a happy child.

In this chapter we offer some parenting techniques that are useful for older babies and toddlers. We will show how to create an atmosphere that fosters your child's development and makes your job easier. Our goals are to make your living area a safe and fun place for him to be and your life with him as rewarding and enjoyable as possible.

Babyproofing

As soon as your child begins to move about the floor, you'll need to eliminate the hazards that he can reach. Babyproofing your home allows him to explore his environment safely. If you do the job well, you won't have to hover over him and he'll have the freedom of movement which is essential for his development. His confidence and independence will increase if you are calm and confident in the experiments he is working on. He'll still need you to supervise him, but you won't have to keep jumping to his rescue.

Remember that babyproofing is not a substitute for supervision.

There's more to babyproofing than removing things that are hazards to him. Keepsakes, valuables and collectibles may not necessarily harm him: he's the one who can harm *them!* If you take the philosophical position that he should learn not to touch certain items in the room, you will be constantly hovering and reprimanding him when he touches something he shouldn't. You will be forced to use a sharp tone of voice, which should be reserved for times when he is truly at risk of endangering himself.

Instead of trying to teach him arbitrary rules, simply remove these things from his reach. Substitute toys, old magazines, junk mail and family photographs in sturdy plastic frames.

Routine Investigations

SHIFTING SCHEDULES

As your newborn baby settles in, you and he struggle to find a suitable routine for his eating and sleeping. It is a process that engrosses all of you in the first weeks. While you learn to decipher your baby's crying into an exposition of his needs, he is busy organizing his feelings of hunger and tiredness. The success of your ministrations increases in direct proportion to how well he understands what he wants.

In a matter of months your baby grows up. He needs less sleep during the day, but sleeps longer at night. He adds solid food to his diet and establishes three meals a day along with two additional bottles or nursings each day.

This shift in routine happens gradually and sometimes there is a lag time between a change in his need for sleep or food and your awareness of it. To minimize the confusion of this restructuring, you must be alert to his signals.

Here's how it can happen:

One morning he may resist going down for his usual nap. You put him in his crib as usual and he objects strenuously. You are puzzled at this behavior, but convinced he needs his rest. In an effort to make him nap you leave him in his crib for awhile. He continues his protests and finally you rescue him. You are frustrated because you know that because he didn't nap, he will be cranky all morning. And as the morning unfolds, your prediction comes true: He gets tired and out of sorts long before lunchtime. You remain convinced that it would have been better if he had slept.

A BABYPROOFING PRIMER

Every home has hazards and you must detect both the obvious and the less obvious dangers both inside and outside.

Indoors

Here are some common safety measures to take:

- Cap or cover used and unused electrical outlets.
- Hide electrical wires under rugs or behind furniture. If there are exposed wires you can't put out of reach, tape them to the floor and wall. Unplug small appliances in kitchen and bathroom and put them away when not in use.
- Lock harmful chemicals in the bathroom, kitchen, garage and basement in a cabinet a child cannot possibly reach.
- Place pressure-mounted safety gates at the top and bottom of stairways and in doorways of other rooms where you don't want your baby to explore.
- Install a safety gate or lock the doors of potentially dangerous rooms like the kitchen, bathroom and laundry room.
- Anchor or remove furniture that can be pulled down or pushed over.
- Remove sharp or breakable items on tables and on the floor.

Outdoors

Here are some areas to check for hazards:

- *Almost everything in the garage or tool shed* (Lock up all gardening and handyman tools, lawn chemicals, weed killer, a gasoline can, etc.)
- Swimming pools, ponds or other nearby water
- Barbecues and related equipment, like lighter fluid and charcoal
- Landscaping ledges, boulders and border fences
- Concrete and stone steps
- Wooden staircases without protective risers
- Sliding glass doors (Put a row of decals down low so your child can see them, and use the lock to keep doors closed.)
- Fences in disrepair
- Unsafe play set or swing
- Uneven sidewalks

Only you can assess the dangers around your house. As your child grows the hazards will change. You must reassess the situation regularly.

The next day the pattern of protest repeats itself. You have two alternatives:

1. You can try to force him to nap, or
2. You can accept the fact that he is giving up the nap and change your routine accordingly.

The first option is a declaration of war which no one will win. The second one is a realistic and sensitive reaction to his growing up. To help him during this period of transition you can either plan outings or other pleasant diversions during the morning, or replace his nap with a quiet time in his crib or playpen. If you try the "time alone to play" strategy, he'll pick up on the change in your attitude and may welcome a chance to be on his own.

A PROPER BALANCE

Learn to gauge the best times of day for different types of activities. Most children benefit from a mix of active and quiet games and play. They need fresh air every day and, as soon as they learn to walk, a safe place to run and play. And except on frigid winter days when the temperature is sub-zero, you'll want to venture outside with him in tow.

Staying inside is anathema to parents with small children. When the weather is cold or inclement, plan to visit a friend who lives nearby or go to a museum. Call ahead of time to find out the museum's policy on visits by small children. Some museums frown on strollers in their halls and require you to check them; others are leery of children on the loose and require them to be in a front or back carrier. If there is a child-oriented museum in your area, you will probably find it to be one of the most accommodating and enjoyable places you can visit.

BEDTIME PRACTICES

Your child may not be ready to go to bed when you think he should be. He may have an inner clock that doesn't wind down until later. He is cheerful and perky when other babies are already asleep. If his inability to go to sleep—or stay asleep—is relatively recent, he may be having troubles elsewhere in his life. We will address this type of sleep problem in Chapter 15.

But if he has been this way since his early babyhood, you'll probably have to accept the fact that he is a night person. And though you can't change his biological clock, you *can* follow a strategy to help you cope with his wakefulness.

1. Establish a quiet time at night: When you are ready for him to disappear, read him a story, cuddle him and then put him in his crib with a toy and leave a small light on. Tell him he can play quietly and that you will be in the next room (or downstairs).
2. Leave the door open so that he can hear the noises of the household and call to you if he wants to hear the reassurance of your voice. *Tell him, though, that you will not come to him and pick him up.*
3. When he gets sleepy, you can come to him on tiptoe to give him a reassuring pat on the back, turn off the play light and turn

on the night light. If the sight of you gets him started again, you may have to stay away and let him put himself to sleep.

MEALTIME STRATEGIES

As your child enters his second year he will begin to feed himself finger foods and spoon soft food from a bowl. You may be amazed at all the places the food can go *besides* his mouth. You'll find it all over his face, in his hair, on his lap, not to mention the walls and floor. Though it may be tempting to feed him yourself to circumvent the mess, he may resent your interference and demand to do it himself.

TIP: Let him feed himself as much as he wants to. Babies are pretty much wash-and-wear creatures. If you use sturdy plastic bibs, line the walls with a clear, washable plastic and put a layer of newspaper under the high chair every day, clean-up won't be too difficult.

Sometimes mealtime is more like playtime. If he doesn't like what you give him, if he isn't hungry, or if he sits with his food too long, he'll lose interest in eating and begin to mash or throw his food.

THE GOLDEN RULE: Give him food he likes, when he's hungry, in the right amounts, for the right amount of time.

A PREDICTABLE LIFE

We have said that both you and your baby will be in better moods if you maintain a routine that is suited to his body rhythm and personality. This type of scheduling promotes his development and adjustment to the world. If his life is predictable, he can identify salient factors in his environment and put them together like a jigsaw puzzle. The world begins to make sense and he learns confidence as an actor on its stage. By doing the same things in the same way every day, you are using repetition as a teaching tool.

If his life isn't predictable, it will take much longer for him to identify and understand what is going on around him. And in extreme cases he might become maladjusted and very unhappy indeed.

OUT OF THE ORDINARY

There are times when your daily life will be altered. You will go on vacation (his life will be disrupted whether you take him or leave him home). You will take a day trip somewhere. You will have long-lost friends staying for awhile as guests. Holiday time, special occasions and illness will disrupt the schedule you follow so carefully. Often the routine isn't the only thing that changes in these circumstances: Your attention can be diverted as well. (There's one notable exception: When your baby is sick, your attention will be riveted on him, of course.) You are distracted and your baby knows it. As a result, he may show his displeasure by being cranky and sleeping or eating poorly.

It is no easy task to handle these temporary interruptions. It would be less than realistic to suggest that you shouldn't travel or celebrate a family wedding. Though there is no perfect solution other than the end of the special event and returning to normal, here are some tips which may help in various situations.

PREP TALK

Prepare your child for the events in his life, both large and small. Whether you are describing a part of your normal routine or an out-of-the-ordinary event, your child is helped by knowing what

---

HANDLING VARIATIONS FROM ROUTINE

- Give your baby your full attention when he eats and at bedtime.
- If it is practical, keep him near you while you are otherwise occupied. Being near you can help reassure him.
- If you must hire a sitter, make sure he knows the person beforehand. If you are to be gone all day or longer, talk to him on the phone.
- If you are traveling with him overnight, stay close to him and pack a few of his favorite toys and comforter. Mementos of home and your proximity will help him adjust.

---

to expect next. Telling him in simple terms what is about to happen reassures him and gives him confidence.

This is especially true of new and unusual events. For example, if you tell him you are going on a car ride to the airport and that you will see airplanes there and will bring a new friend home (your Aunt Matilda), he will be excited about riding in the car and seeing the planes, and will show less concern that there is a stranger riding in the car on the way home.

Becoming a Sibling

When you anticipate your second child, preparing your first one for the new baby's arrival is a top priority. If your older child is in his second year, his comprehension of this momentous event will be limited. Before the baby actually comes, your child will have only a vague concept of what is happening to him. All he really knows is that whatever it is, it's important.

Even though your older child may be quite little when your second child is born, there are some steps you can take to help him adjust.

BEFORE THE NEW BABY IS BORN

- Tell him that a baby is growing in Mommy's uterus. Don't say "tummy"—if he thinks a baby can grow in a stomach, he may stop eating to prevent a baby from growing in *his* stomach. Explain that, when the time comes, the baby is going to live with your family. Don't belabor the points or overcomplicate the discussion.

- Give him a rubber baby doll to play with and take care of.

- Include him in the preparations for the baby. As you prepare the nursery, talk about where the baby is going to sleep and where big brother sleeps. Make sure he understands that he will continue to have a place in the house even after the baby arrives.

- When your wife's due date approaches, explain that Mommy must go to a hospital to have the baby and that she will stay there a couple of days. Emphasize that you will be at home to take care of him until she comes back and (if the hospital allows sibling visits) that you will bring him to visit her there. If the hospital policy doesn't allow such visits, your wife should promise to call and talk to him every day.

- If you are working away from home, try to arrange for paternity leave from your job. If this is impossible, arrange for someone he already knows to take care of him. It is best if he can remain in his own home and not be shuttled off to Grandma's. If he is away from home, he may fear that the new baby is replacing him while he's gone.

- Buy a supply of small presents for Mommy to give him when he visits the hospital. If he can't visit, she can send a small present home each day with you.

AFTER THE NEW BABY COMES

- If possible, include your older child in the baby's homecoming.

- When you bring the new baby home, both you and your wife should plan to devote as much of your attention to your older child as possible. The baby won't notice if you feed her and read to the other child at the same time. She has never known a world without a sibling; he has.

- Plan a few special excursions with your older child and leave the baby with a sitter.

- Don't be surprised or angry when your older child expresses his wish that the baby go away. It doesn't usually take long before your older child figures out that the baby distracts you and interferes with your attention to him.

- Make a point of praising your older child's toddler accomplishments. Comment about how little the new baby can do compared to him. (The baby doesn't know the difference, but your toddler will burst his buttons.) Once your older child sees that the baby can't do much of anything, he'll feel less threatened. All will go well until your younger child starts to walk and talk. When the second child begins to "perform," the older child feels threatened again. Always make sure that your older child has special "grown-up" things to do that set him apart from the baby.

- Encourage him to help you care for the baby by bringing you a diaper or doing some other simple task.

- Be vigilant to ensure that your child doesn't endanger the baby by feeding her a nonedible lunch or otherwise hurting her. Don't assume that he is going to hurt the baby, but be *ready to intervene.* A kiss can turn into a bite, a pat can become a hit, a hug can be too tight.

SAFETY TIP: Never leave your baby and toddler unattended together.

Your Young Creative Person

All this talk about routines and scheduling doesn't mean that you and your baby should be acting like robots. Quite the opposite. Be as creative as you can with him and think up ways to foster his imagination and ingenuity.

EVERYDAY PLAY

The easiest way to develop your child's creativity is to offer him a wide variety of playthings. Though the stores are full of toys that will stretch your child's abilities, some of the best diversions come from your own closets and shelves. Even very young children like to play dress-up and explore the interiors of cabinets and closets.

As we discussed in the *Babyproofing* section (pages 140-43), you must lock up or otherwise remove anything that could harm your child as well as items you want to protect. But while you are clearing away these items, remember to replace them with as many safe playthings as possible.

FINDING SOLUTIONS

One of the major tasks of an older baby and toddler is to learn to be self-sufficient. Your child must feed himself, master a spoon, get dressed and undressed, maneuver buttons and zippers, and so on. These efforts to gain independence from you are excruciatingly difficult for him. His fingers are awkward and every detail of these operations is a struggle. Though he will learn by watching what you do, he will still have to devise his own methods of achieving his goals. Using trial and error, he will slowly solve each problem in turn.

Because these efforts are so time-consuming, you will often have to take over and do them for him. Your own patience level and the reality that you cannot spend all day getting him dressed, will dictate that you step in. But remember that, ultimately, he must learn to do these things for himself—and that, as we'll discuss in the next chapter, he may object strenuously to your interference.

TIP: Never underestimate the power of praise. Rejoice with your child whenever he accomplishes even the smallest step toward a goal.

Patience, Please

The most important part of day-to-day parenting is being patient with your child. It is also probably the hardest part. Every parent must work on being calm and unhurried. It will be easier to have patience if you look at the world from your child's point of view. So let's take some time now and explore your child's tasks, needs and fears.

13

Personal Differences

Who *is* this child of yours? How do you relate to one another? These are two questions that are important to consider during your child's turbulent second year. In fact, we can extend the ancient Greek philosophy and urge you to "Know your child, and her stage of development."

Your child's temperament and personality, and how it meshes with your own, determines a great deal about how you live together. Now that she is entering the so-called Terrible Twos, it is more important than ever to understand her point of view and how it clashes with yours. Knowing who she is, where she is in her development, and how you fit together will help you cope when the urge to push comes to shove.

The value of analyzing your relationship depends on the type of child you have. If she is adaptable, predictable and easy to please, you won't have much cause for interpersonal diplomacy. But if she is at some other point on the spectrum of relationships, which most children are (at least temporarily) in their second year, you may find that understanding who she is and reviewing your own motives and attitudes will help you settle your set-tos amicably—and may also defuse some more serious confrontations.

In this chapter we will describe how a typical toddler views the world. We'll discuss the Terrible Twos, the range of natural temperamental traits in children and the way parents typically react.

Once you can step back from this period of conflicts and power struggles and analyze it properly, you'll be able to stretch your patience further than before. And with your help she'll return to being reasonable sooner rather than later.

The State of Toddlerhood

Before we discuss specific traits, let's examine the maturation level of the toddler. It's an odd transitional time when your child is no longer a baby, nor is she a preschooler. The period is analogous to adolescence, which transforms a child into an adult. Just as the teen years are difficult for child and parent, so is toddlerhood. Both are periods marked with struggle and conflict as the child breaks away from parental dominance.

In order to separate from you, your child must strike out on her own—do things *her* way. She is inexperienced, and her ideas have little or no reference to what is best for her. Indeed, what she wants to do may be completely illogical. As an adult, you know how something should be done, and in the old days she would let you have your way. No longer. So the stage is now set for battle.

She waves the red flag and you start to match wills. . . . But wait a minute!

Look again at who you're fighting. This is no formidable foe, just a grown-up baby. Though she walks, talks and understands what you say to her, she's really an impostor. She doesn't have any of the perspective or understanding that an older child has.

TODDLER TIME

Your toddler lives in the present.

Though she remembers dramatic events in her life, such as a fall from her crib or a traumatic visit to the doctor, she doesn't have a developed sense of the past. To her the past is what happened five minutes ago and the future is what you tell her is going to happen next. She is only dimly aware that time is passing.

She is oblivious of the adult values that are associated with time.

She won't heed your admonitions about being in a hurry. In fact, she may dawdle just because you are so actively interested in her hurrying up. She is breaking away from you and the only way she knows how to declare her independence is to do the opposite of what you want.

She can't think very far ahead.

For example, suppose you are going on an outing and you ask her if she would like a drink before you leave. She shakes her head to indicate "No," and off you go to the park. Five minutes after you leave, she says she is thirsty and wants a drink. Unless you know why she "changes her mind," this reversal can be *very* irritating. You might even wonder if she does it on purpose. The logical move is simply to get in the habit of bringing a drink and a snack with you wherever you go.

PUBLIC APPEARANCE

Just as she has little sense of time, she has almost no understanding of social grace.

Even though she can be winning enough to charm birds out of the trees when she wants to, she can throw a tantrum in the same setting minutes later. Her enchanting ways are meant to draw attention and approval to herself. But if she is thwarted in some way, she'll discard the charm and switch to another, much less endearing voice. This behavior is particularly distressing in public and whenever you are anxious to impress extended family and friends. When the storm clouds burst, quickly and calmly remove her from the scene.

CAUSE AND EFFECT

She can't anticipate the result of her actions.

This, of course, is one reason you were so busy babyproofing your home in the last chapter. But this inability to predict what will happen goes beyond safety around the house. When, for example, your child insists on running away from you in a public place, she can't and won't understand that she may get lost. In her mind she is simply exploring the area and getting some exercise. No amount of patient explanation or yelling will hinder a wandering child. In this instance, a harness or other restraint is your only recourse.

CROSS PURPOSES

She is self-centered in the extreme and dedicated to satisfying her own needs and wants.

She doesn't understand or care that her insistence on getting herself dressed in the morning will make you late for work. After all, *she* doesn't have to be on time. Her job in life is to learn how to be self-sufficient. The demands of the outside world remain outside her understanding. In her eyes your existence is still anchored in the ways you can help her achieve her goals.

What do you do if she insists on dressing herself in spite of the fact that you have to drop her off at the sitter on your way to work, and that you'll be late as a result? You have a couple of choices:

1. Get her started on the project much earlier in the morning, or

2. Drop her off in her pajamas with her clothes for the day in a bag. She can spend the day getting dressed *there!*

Much of the struggle during this difficult year comes when you and she are working at cross purposes. She cannot put herself in your shoes and negotiate. In our example, your rushing to work interferes with her learning to dress herself and both of you are determined to win.

So instead of doing battle with her, you have to handle her and her willful ideas. As the adult on the case, it is your job to find a suitable solution to both your problem and hers. In our two suggested solutions offered above, both of you get what you want without expecting too much of her abilities.

REMEMBER: No solution, no matter how creative it is, will work if you ask her to do what she is as yet incapable of doing.

Individual Temperaments

As if it isn't enough to struggle along with the developmental limitations of being a toddler, a child's individual traits can add to an already unstable situation. In their excellent book, *The Difficult Child* (New York: Bantam, 1985), Dr. Stanley Turecki and Leslie Tonner outline a constellation of nine characteristics of a child's natural behavior or temperament. These were first defined by Drs. Alexander Thomas, Stella Chess, and Herbert Birch of New York University. In 1956, these three scholars began the New York Longitudinal Study, an ongoing project which is following the lives of 133 people from infancy to young adulthood. The study is tracking each individual's temperament as he or she interacts with the environment.

Here's how Turecki and Tonner explain the nine traits:

1. ACTIVITY LEVEL. How active is the child generally, from an early age?
2. DISTRACTIBILITY. How easily is the child distracted? Can he pay attention?
3. PERSISTENCE. Does the child stay with something he likes? How persistent or stubborn is he when he wants something? [In their book, the authors group persistence with adaptability and, for clarity's sake, so shall we.]
4. ADAPTABILITY. How does the child deal with transition and change?
5. APPROACH/WITHDRAWAL. What is the child's initial response to newness—new places, people, foods, clothes?
6. INTENSITY. How loud is the child generally, whether happy or unhappy?
7. REGULARITY. How predictable is the child in his patterns of sleep, appetite, bowel habits?
8. SENSORY THRESHOLD. How does the child react to sensory stimuli: noise, bright lights, colors, smells, pain, warm weather, tastes, the texture and feel of clothes? Is he easily bothered? Is he easily overstimulated?
9. MOOD. What is the child's basic mood? Do positive or negative reactions predominate?

According to these researchers, any child can be analyzed using these yardsticks. An "easy" child has low levels of activity, distractibility and intensity. She adapts well, approaches rather than

TRAITS THAT MAKE A CHILD HARD TO MANAGE

The child may be:

- active, perhaps to the point of being wild and out of control.
- easily distractible and unable to concentrate even for a moment.
- loud, whether she is happy or angry.
- sensitive to stimulus: she reacts strongly to the slightest discomfort and is easily overstimulated.
- resistant to change and adapts poorly when she must alter her life. She reacts negatively when she must start or finish an activity. She fixes on certain foods, clothes and toys and won't accept variety. When she wants something, she stubbornly whines or nags until she gets what she wants.
- reluctant to accept new people and places. She will withdraw or cling.
- generally unpredictable. Her appetite and need for sleep are erratic and she is willful about when and how much she eats and sleeps. She has an uneven and changeable disposition to match.
- negative or serious and, in contrast with other children, seems basically unhappy. She doesn't express pleasure easily.

withdraws from new things and has predictable personal habits. Her sensory threshold is high and her mood is generally positive.

On the other end of the spectrum we find the "difficult" child, the types of children about whom Turecki and Tonner wrote their book. Though there is no stereotype of a hard-to-manage child, she has more traits that are the opposite of the easy child.

Turecki and Tonner estimate that there are 2 to 3 million very difficult children in the United States and many more who have difficult features. Most children fall somewhere in the middle of the spectrum between easy and difficult. Your child may show one or more difficult traits to a greater or lesser degree.

Often these characteristics go hand in hand. A child's adaptability and approach/withdrawal relates to her acceptance of new people, places and things. Her activity level can connect to her intensity level; her sensitivity to stimulation can aggravate her ability to concentrate.

Is It Temporary Or Permanent?

Nearly every toddler is difficult. It's a normal, predictable stage of toddler development. Somewhere in the second year they show streaks of willfulness and stubbornness. As a group they tend to be negative and explosively emotional. How can you tell if your child is truly difficult or simply going through the difficult stage otherwise known as the Terrible Twos? To find out the answer, ask yourself the following:

First, has she always been like this? A difficult child has also had a difficult babyhood: Was she irregular in her demands for bottle or breast? Did she have trouble sleeping through the night? Were her sleep habits hard to regulate? Was she very active, fussy, grumpy or loud? Was she a jumpy baby, as we described in Chapter 11? What was her reaction to new people, places and things?

Second, is there any recent change in her life that might cause difficult behavior? If she has been ill, if you are going through a traumatic experience like divorce, if she suddenly has a new sibling to cope with, she could well become difficult. Stress can affect your child's behavior, but it won't necessarily alter her temperament. When the transition is made, or if the problem is suddenly solved, she will become more reasonable once again.

If the answers are basically "No" to all of the above, then you can be assured that you are in a temporary tempest. Just hold on tight and you'll make it through the storm virtually unscathed.

If, however, you find yourself nodding your head to questions about her infancy, then you'll be spending more time at sea. Instead of months, you are probably looking at years. Take heart, however, from the fact that children who are difficult or unusual often become rather remarkable adults. According to Turecki and Tonner, Eleanor Roosevelt, Albert Einstein, Thomas Edison, Pablo Picasso and Winston Churchill all fall into this category—a distinguished group for your child to be associated with, don't you think? Later in life, your child's difficult traits will quite likely turn into very positive ones and help her to succeed where others may fail.

Whether you are in it for the short or long term, there are ways to cope. We will describe them fully in the next chapter and help you deal effectively with toddler-adult confrontations.

How You and Your Child Fit Together

In their book, Turecki and Tonner talk about parent-child relationships in terms of two kinds of fit: emotional and behavioral. How well you and your child fit together will help determine your attitude toward her. Every child and parent is different, which makes it hard to establish any hard-and-fast rules. But, in general, the easier the child is, the more positive your reaction will be to her and the better the two of you will fit.

EMOTIONAL FIT

If you *like* your child (as distinct from loving her) and feel comfortable with her, you and she have a good emotional fit. In evaluating your attitude toward your child it is important to separate like from love. Most parents love their children but they don't always like their children uniformly. Not every trait, after all, is likeable—some are pluses, others are minuses. All will be well, however, if there are as many positive signs as there are negative ones.

As an example, it is hard to like your toddler's stubborn willfulness and refusal to be reasonable. But she probably has other personality or temperamental traits that you do like which balance the scale. You may appreciate her industrious efforts at independence and marvel at her patience with trial-and-error learning. And remember those birds she charmed out of the trees? You are probably one of those that eat out of her hand from time to time.

BEHAVIORAL FIT

This is an assessment of your child's behavior and how well it fits with your lifestyle and emotional makeup. If, for example, you are very neat and dislike it when your house is in disarray, you will have problems coping with a very active child. A child like this can completely ransack a room in a matter of minutes. Like

STRATEGIES FOR HANDLING AN ACTIVE CHILD

1. Beef up your babyproofing.
2. Make one room in your house a knockabout playroom. Remove all the small mess-making items (books, throw pillows, bric-a-brac, etc.) except toys and other playthings. If possible, locate the play space in a well-trafficked area, so that it will be convenient for indoor playtime while you are on the phone, making dinner, etc.
3. Make it a policy to pick up only one time, at the end of the day. If once isn't enough, add another clean-up time before lunch.
4. Harness some of your child's energy and enlist her help during clean-up. Make it a game and she'll probably think it is great fun.
5. Get out of the house more often and for longer periods of time. Make plans even on cold and rainy days. In a manner of speaking, you need to "walk the dog."
6. Arrange play dates with other toddlers. Though you'll have to live through the chaos when it's your turn to host, you will come home to a neat house on the days when you and your child are guests over there.

the mythical Sisyphus who was doomed to roll a rock up a hill only to have it roll down again, you will be endlessly putting away and cleaning up after your toddler.

If there's a discrepancy between how you want your child to act and how she actually behaves, see if you can't lessen the gap by changing her environment and revising your tactics. You may be surprised at how creative you are at finding solutions. The old saw that necessity is the mother of invention was probably coined by a parent.

The Good-Enough Parent

In the face of human frailties and the difficult dynamics we've discussed that relate to toddler development, the job of parenting can be a genuine challenge. But don't worry. You'll be doing great if you just do the best you can. The way you fit together won't be perfect. Nor does it matter that you aren't perfect parents, nor that she isn't a perfect child.

Many experts agree that doing your best, usually referred to as "good-enough" parenting, is all that's needed. From the beginning it's a natural process of child teaching parent and vice versa. You select tactics and methods that work and reject those that don't. She learns to understand who you are and what you expect of her.

This evolution begins when your child is born and continues through babyhood and toddlerhood. Over time, you learn to be a parent who generally reacts appropriately and who is adept at finding workable solutions. For her part, your child comes into her own as she breaks free of limitations as a toddler and enters the fullness of childhood. As you graduate from the Terrible Twos, one thing is certain—neither you nor she will ever be the same.

Now that we have analyzed the toddler dilemma and examined its prickly thorns, let's look more closely at ways of handling it—carefully.

14

Toddler Tactics

Just as there is debate between optimists and pessimists as to whether a glass is half full or half empty, a case can be made that toddlerhood is as much the Terrific Twos as it is the Terrible Twos. Every child, even the most Terrible Two, has endearing qualities, habits and mannerisms.

Your child's naïveté is enchanting, his energy remarkable. He's a half-pint of potential, charm and good humor. When he's in this mode, there's nothing to do except relax and enjoy it. Then, when the other side of him appears and your child starts acting horribly, remembering the wonderful aspects of his personality will help you cope with the unpleasantness. Enjoy his happy times and store up some fuel for the less happy ones.

In the previous chapter, we talked about your toddler's temperament, personality and developmental level. Let's look at some of his less acceptable behavior in the context of his individual characteristics, and discuss effective management techniques that will help you handle it.

What Does He Do That Drives You Crazy?

To get an overview of where your problems lie, set aside a few days and observe your child. Jot down his behavior that irritates you and the way you react to him. When compiling your list, note the type of behavior (whining, having tantrums, hitting, etc.), the issue of the dispute, the situation that sparked it, the time of day it usually occurs, and the setting where it takes place. And, finally, it is especially important to observe how you respond to the confrontation and whether your response was effective.

The goal in making a list like this is to look for patterns in your interactions. Identifying similarities in his misbehavior will help you focus on appropriate and effective actions. It will also help you decide which behavioral problems need your attention first. Because there are so many interwoven parts of any parent-child interaction, we suggest that you fill out a grid-like chart (there are some sample charts in the Appendix), and then analyze it in the light of what follows.

Each variable in the chart can be an important clue. Let's take each in turn and examine some of the conclusions and solutions you may come to in each case.

TYPE OF BEHAVIOR

Ask yourself how unacceptable is his behavior in each case. Not all behavior is equal: While whining is irritating, it doesn't hurt anyone. Biting, slapping, hitting and pinching are much worse because they encroach on another person's space and may hurt as well. Analyzing and rating each type of behavior in these terms will help you focus on the task of behavior modification that lies ahead. The more unacceptable the behavior is, the higher priority it has.

THE ISSUE/SITUATION

Though there are many issues which can provoke a toddler, two of the most common have to do with control and independence.

TIP: Never make a strong stand on an unimportant issue.

"DO IT MYSELF" comes up when your child is learning self-sufficiency in his everyday routines. We touched upon one example of this in Chapter 13, when we described the child who insists on dressing herself in the morning. We suggested solutions which would enable her to work at learning without interfering with your schedule.

Your child will demand this right in other phases of his daily life, too. Let's move to the kitchen and describe another example. Suppose that your child refuses to eat his meals. We'll assume that you follow the golden rule in Chapter 12 and offer him food he likes in the proper amount at the right time. But because you can't stand the mess he makes when he feeds himself, you prefer to feed him yourself. He systematically turns his head away as you offer him spoonfuls of his favorite foods.

What's up? He resents your interference with the spoon and is asserting his right to feed himself. When you offer him the chance to do it himself, his interest in food will probably return.

TIP: To minimize the mess, change his diet to finger foods which don't require a spoon. When you offer him soft foods to spoon, put very little in the bowl until he improves his skill.

"DO IT MY WAY" is related to the first type of assertiveness, but it is often less rational and therefore more irritating to a parent. It is clearly a declaration of independence, toddler style. Examples of this issue can be sprinkled throughout your toddler's life. Toilet training is a classic situation that can involve his refusal to do what you want him to. As we suggested earlier, he'll be out of diapers more quickly if you take your own interests out of the equation.

TIP: Let him do it his way unless it does him harm or endangers him, or interferes with your life.

TIMING

If, for example, he has more blowups in the late afternoon, he may simply have run out of steam. Another possibility is that he may be overstimulated and cranky after a long day of play. This is where your understanding of his personality comes in. If it seems appropriate, give him a nutritious snack, like cheese and crackers, to bridge the gap until dinnertime. If you suspect that he is wound up too tight, make the late afternoon a quiet time when you read to him.

Another typical situation related to timing is his need for your attention. Suppose your child starts acting up every time you (1) sit down to feed your second child, (2) talk on the phone, (3) entertain guests, or (4) try to have a conversation with your wife. He is jealous and seeks your attention, even if it is negative.

TIP: When you see a pattern like this developing, stop what you are doing. Tell your child that you know he wants your attention but that he has to wait awhile, and that he can sit on your lap or next to you in the meantime. Knowing that you know what his problem is and being physically close to you will help him settle down.

WHERE

When he goes to play group, does he consistently hit other children or throw toys around angrily? If so, he may not be ready handle the give-and-take of playing with his peers. Even though toddlers don't really play together and instead play side by side, they still must share toys and be willing to take turns. You may have to take him out of the group for a few months until he is more mature emotionally. During this period you should play games with him that require sharing and turns. He will accept from you what he won't from his contemporaries.

Does he throw tantrums in a movie theater or in the supermarket? First, look for the possible causes of the behavior. Public places can be difficult for a child who is either easily overstimulated, or very active and wants to run around and touch everything. If he can't deal with all that he sees and hears, his only recourse and release is to have an emotional eruption. Equally, an active and impulsive child will resent the restraints you put on him and will tell you just how he feels about it.

In either case your course of action is the same.

1. Keep your visits to places like these short and low-key.

2. Take him out of the store if a tantrum erupts. Don't be tempted to return with him minutes later to finish your errand.

3. Make it a rule not to take him with you when you do the grocery shopping, or go to a fancy restaurant. You deserve time away from him and peace while doing your major chores.

YOUR RESPONSE AND WHAT HAPPENED NEXT

Looking at these two variables together will help you assess how effective your tactics are. If your response has no results and the answer to "What happened next" is that the behavior continued or actually worsened, then you need to rethink your plan of attack.

When the problem either remains the same or escalates, the chances are your response has been emotional and inappropriate. An appropriate response, as we shall see in the next section, is one in which you think rather than emote.

Another question to ask yourself: "Did I follow through?" Consistency—doing what you say—is a very important part of getting results.

Let's take an example: Your child is throwing food on the floor and you warn him that if he does it again, you are going to take away his bowl or plate. He looks at you knowingly and repeats the game. It is obvious he is testing you. If, instead of carrying out the warning, you respond by sitting down with him and taking over the spoon because you really want him to eat something, he'll ignore your warnings in the future.

TIP: Never threaten what you aren't willing to follow through on. When you take a stand, always do what you say you are going to do.

Learning to Respond

In their book *The Difficult Child,* Dr. Stanley Turecki and Leslie Tonner outline a method that enables parents to respond to difficult children in appropriate and effective ways. This is a sequence of six steps which is useful for *all* parents to follow when a child is acting unacceptably. Let's look at the way they describe this step-by-step process and add a discussion of how each part helps you interact effectively with your child.

STEP 1: CAN I DEAL WITH IT?

Remember always: If you can't deal with it, disengage.

The first step is to ask yourself how *you* are feeling at the moment. If you are in a bad mood or feeling nervous or upset, you probably shouldn't try to cope with the situation. Your patience is low and your emotions are ragged; you simply don't have the capacity for an appropriate response.

In order to respond to your child properly, you must leave your emotional baggage on the sidelines. If you are not able to do so, you may make matters worse. The problem may very well escalate to worse misbehavior and an increase in your ill will. You may say or do something you later wish you hadn't.

How do you do nothing when something must be done? Disengage yourself and your child from the situation. If he is acting up in public, take him away. You probably shouldn't say much more than a simple "Okay, we're leaving." Don't create a cycle of threatening and then relenting. Do what you say you are going to do with as little fanfare as you can manage.

If you are at home, stop your child's behavior and then disengage yourself. If, for example, your child is throwing his toys or his food, end the session, pick him up and put him in his room or some other safe area. Remain at a distance from him for a little while until both of you calm down. If he is having trouble calming down, take him in your arms and cuddle him. Snuggling can help both of you feel better.

When your mood causes the behavior: Cuddling is especially useful if your child's behavior is triggered by *your* mood. If you are distracted and concentrating on a problem quite apart from him, he knows he'll be able to regain your attention if he does something you don't want him to do. Children always try for attention—even if it's negative.

Another possibility is that your behavior makes him worried or nervous and, therefore, more prone to anger or emotional displays. He needs you to be cool, calm and collected. When he intuits that something is wrong, he needs reassurance. A hug and a kiss can help both of you.

NOTE: If you *can* deal with it, proceed to the next step.

STEP 2: BECOME THE LEADER

Remember always: Be neutral—don't respond emotionally.

In this step, you remember that you are an adult and in charge of your parent-child relationship. This is when you rid yourself of the feeling that you are a victim of your child's behavior or that he is somehow master of the situation. Remember that he is really just a grown-up baby with limitations and developmental immaturity. You are the boss.

STEP 3: "FRAME" THE BEHAVIOR

Remember always: Look at behavior, not motives.

Here you put into play the behavioral chart that we described at the beginning of this chapter. Your observations help you recognize the current problem as a part of a pattern. If you are familiar with his behavior, you can "deal with it" better; surprises are much harder to handle effectively.

STEP 4: IS IT TEMPERAMENT?

Remember always: If it's temperament, manage.

This step is the crossroads when you must decide if the child can help what he is doing. In the effort to decide whether the child is acting deliberately or involuntarily, we would add another aspect to Dr. Turecki's question and ask: *"Is it developmental?"*

If your child's behavior is caused by either his temperament or his developmental immaturity, you will naturally be sympathetic and help him to manage his temperament and his limitations. Punishment is inappropriate and, as we discussed in Chapter 13, you should handle the matter diplomatically.

First, look your child in the eye (to make sure he is listening) and interpret his problem to him verbally in a way he can under-

HOW TO TEMPER TEMPER

There are two types of temper tantrums: manipulative and temperamental. The former is sparked when your child doesn't get his way, the latter springs from traits of temperament that lie within. The first kind does not kindle much, if any, sympathy in you, while the second does. The latter type is usually more intense and usually lasts longer.

When your child starts having a tantrum, you need to step back and analyze which kind of an outburst he is displaying. Once you have decided, here's how to play it:

Handling a Manipulative Outburst

Adopt a firm attitude that he may not do or have what he wants. You must communicate to him that he can't get his way by being a pest. Tell him No and try to distract him with something that is completely off the point. If that doesn't work, ignore him as much as you can. If he begins to harm or endanger himself, you must intervene. Stay firm and don't back down.

Handling a Temperamental Outburst

Your attitude is somewhat different for this type of tantrum. Because you realize that he can't really help it, you are naturally more sympathetic and reassuring. But these tantrums are more intense and your child has a greater chance of hurting himself, so you will need to be physically close to him. Hold him if he will allow you to. Stay calm and tell him you know he is upset, but that he will feel better soon.

Sometimes you can distract him with a toy or a book. You can also try patting or rubbing his back, or singing to him, as well as sponging his face with a damp washcloth. Trial and error will help you find what is soothing to your distraught child.

stand, a technique that Turecki and Tonner call "labeling." This means that you make a statement of fact that does not blame him or accuse him of being bad. Some examples of labeling: "You are

---

The Hybrid Outburst

A tantrum is not necessarily either one type or the other. A manipulative tantrum can slide into a temperamental one when the child gets locked into being upset, and a temperamental outburst can become manipulative when he realizes the power his outburst has over you. In both cases the switch from one to the other is subtle.

To gauge what is happening, you must evaluate the situation and your child. There are no hard-and-fast rules. You are the only one who can know which is which. If you see the nature of the tantrum switching from one type to the other, change your approach accordingly.

---

overexcited." "I know you don't like (*to sit still, new places or people, etc.*)." Once you have stated the situation, you can then proceed to explain what you and he are going to do about it.

STEP 5: IS IT RELEVANT?

Remember always: If it's irrelevant, do as little as possible.

In this step, you are to weed out the behaviors that may irritate you but that don't merit punishment. They are irrelevant and require little response from you. The concept here is to punish only the critical behavior and ignore or respond minimally to everything else. For example, biting is punishable, as is running into the street. By and large, your toddler's irrelevant behavior relates to his stage of development or temperament, which, as we have said, he can't help and you shouldn't punish him for.

STEP 6: EFFECTIVE PUNISHMENT

Remember always: If it's relevant, punish briefly.

Some young children can be punished with a firm reprimand, others need a little more emphasis, but the punishment should *never* be either delayed or extended. In addition to reprimanding your child, you can put him in his room for five minutes or give him an occasional smack on his rear or leg.

At this young age it is important to keep your repertoire simple. Don't embroider elaborate variations of either of these two alternatives. Spending an hour in his room won't teach him the lesson any more effectively. His limited concept of time precludes any connection between the crime and a prolonged punishment. If you feel comfortable with a smack as punishment, use it only for emphasis when he has endangered himself or others. Never hit him hard or slap his face or head. A swat on his diaper carries effective shock value: While it doesn't hurt him, it does make your point.

Spare the Rod and Praise the Child

While punishing your child should be an infrequent event, praising him should be an everyday affair. Praise is a powerful tool of parenting which will help you reinforce your child's good behavior. If he helps you pick up his toys, tell him what a good job he did and celebrate his success by giving him a hug or sharing a cookie and a glass of milk.

As he matures, he will begin to do things for himself and be able to entertain himself while you are otherwise occupied. Watch for signs that he is developing this kind of maturity. Exult in his successes and encourage him when he falters. If you give him a positive self-image and confidence in himself, breaking away from you won't be so difficult and life with your toddler won't be so terrible after all.

Now that we have untangled the knots of his reactive behavior, we are ready to tackle your child's world of fears, anxieties and the other monsters that may lurk under his bed.

15

Dragons to Conquer

P arenting is a balancing act: You must nurture and protect your little one at the very same time you are encouraging her to be independent and capable of caring for herself. You want to foster her innocence and grace, but you also know that she must learn the facts of life. Your child's naïveté endears her to you; it seems a shame that it can't last. This dilemma is as old as time and it is discovered afresh every time a child is born.

You may be concerned about all this, but your child isn't. There's no question in *her* mind about what she should be doing, for she has an inner drive which pushes her to master life. As she explores the world, she gradually loses her innocence. She experiences the joy of success and the frustration of failure, and learns how to handle both disappointment and surprise.

In this chapter we will watch as your child meets the world head on and braves the unknown. We will discuss the fears and anxieties common in early childhood that are natural expressions of these efforts of learning and growing. We'll see how they often manifest themselves, and offer suggestions about some ways you can help your child get through them.

What Is Anxiety?

In her book *The Magic Years* (New York: Charles Scribner's Sons, 1959), author Selma Fraiberg describes anxiety as the way that a child "prepares for 'danger.'" According to Fraiberg, your child's anxiety evolves from the startle reflex she had as a newborn when she would cry if she were handled roughly, heard a loud noise or were blinded by light. The reflex gradually fades. She adjusts to stimulation and learns to enjoy rough-and-tumble games.

As her experience increases, she stops being "shocked" and learns to anticipate something unpleasant. The anxiety your child feels is similar to yours—though, of course, the dangers she wrestles with are very different. You may be worried about paying the rent, while she becomes anxious when she sees you getting dressed in your going-to-work clothes. She learns the signals that say, "I am going to leave you soon."

While the sources of your anxieties often differ, you both may agree that visits to doctors are nerve-racking. Neither one of you may like relative strangers poking about your persons, though when it's your turn, you won't cry and squirm like she does. You are able to distinguish between the significance of a routine checkup and a visit due to illness. If she doesn't like going to the doctor, each visit will be the same to her—equally unpleasant.

Fraiberg states that anxiety "is not a pathological condition in itself but a necessary and normal physiological and mental preparation for danger." It helps the individual survive and lessens the impact of sudden shifts and twists in a child's everyday life. Thus the anxieties of a child are very real and important.

As parents, you will find it helps if you can put aside your adult sophistication and try to understand how she is feeling. It is necessary for a child to be anxious at least some of the time, so you must help her learn how to cope with it. As she grows, she will conquer one dragon and then move on to the next . . . and the next. Before you know it, she'll have discarded the worries of childhood and taken on the grown-up anxieties of getting into college and finding a career.

The Art of Self-Defense

How does your child deal with her anxieties and fears? During her first year she expresses fear by crying or by clinging to you. As she gains experience, though she is still apt to cry and cling at times, she will use her imagination to create other avenues of expression that are more specific and help her pinpoint what she is afraid of.

Imagination is a key weapon in her arsenal of self-defense. It helps the child conquer the source of the problem without ever having to draw blood or throw a punch. Your child can use her imagination in this war with her fears in a variety of ways. She can act out an event with her toys, devise games and routines to rehearse an event that worries her, play dress-up, pretend to be a scary monster, and invent imaginary monsters to fight or an imaginary friend to keep her company.

These harmless but effective methods are spontaneous solutions to the problems of growing up. Your child will select a remedy which is appropriate for a particular anxiety and which fits her personality. Be alert to these imaginary exercises and encourage her efforts to master the "things that go bump in the night."

All will go well when she can apply her imaginary wits to a situation but, unfortunately, there are many childhood fears that a child cannot handle successfully alone. When she can't, and simply tries to avoid whatever it is that she fears, you will *have* to step in to help.

How You Can Help

Your child will signal her fear by adamantly refusing to do something—behavior that you probably associate more closely with the struggle for independence as a Terrible Two. The reason for her negative behavior may not be apparent at first, but often, if you think again, you can find a recent event in her life which will explain her reaction.

You know your child well and how she is waging her fight for independence, so you'll be able to detect the negative behavior which is due to fear. It is important to separate this particular behavior from her regular battles over Toddler Rights, for it must be treated differently.

Once you have identified the source of her fear, you must ease her into dealing with it. Look for some indirect, nonthreatening ways of getting her to approach what she is anxious about. Many times it can be as simple as offering her a chance to play-act whatever is bothering her.

GAMES OF SEPARATION

When she learns to crawl, play chase games with her. This will help her play-act her fears of separation and reassure herself that she *can* return to the safety of your arms. Take turns chasing each other. (If you get on your hands and knees, she'll enjoy the game even more.) When you catch each other, embrace her with a hug. The denouement of reunion is *the* important feature of this game.

Another game in the same vein that she'll like is to run (or crawl) a short distance away from you and then return to your arms in joyful reunion. In this version of the "separation game" she is the one who makes the choice of leaving you and decides just how far she feels safe in going. This is an especially good game for daddies who must leave to go to work every day.

For example, if your child is worried about your leaving her each day for work, she might put your shoes on, pick up your briefcase and say "Bye-bye!" as she staggers around the room.

In the rundown of fears and anxieties that follows we will suggest some more specific ways to help her conquer her fears.

TIP: Stay close to her as she explores the "enemy." Your presence will reassure her and give her the courage to conquer it.

More on Separation

As your baby develops new accomplishments in her first year, like sitting independently, crawling and walking, she may become clingy. Her new ability to leave you upsets her. She may crawl or walk away from you a short distance and then return hurriedly to you with tears of fright.

Her new skills are a huge step in her separation from you; they set her adrift from you. Now there is an ocean of space that can come between you and she is worried about it. Will she lose you? Will you leave her?

SLEEP PROBLEMS

There are many different causes of sleep problems. Teething and intermittent bad dreams are two common culprits. In addition, some children are light or restless sleepers. When your child wakens in the middle of the night, her nursery is dark (even with a night-light) and she may become lonesome and in need of your reassurance.

Not every child has the same intensity of anxiety; some require more attention and awaken more frequently. Handling these interruptions of sleep can be troublesome: Parents can lose both sleep and patience. You may hear tales of woe about letting a child cry himself to sleep at night. This technique is related to a school of thought that was popular in the past—but has since been rejected by experts—which held that you shouldn't comfort your child in the middle of the night. The theory was that she had to cry it out, however long it might take.

Now experts agree that your crying child needs a pat on the back and a few words of comfort. Here are a few other guidelines to follow:

- Before you go to her, be sure that she really is awake and won't settle down and go back to sleep on her own.
- If your first attempt doesn't work, and she resumes crying when you leave, wait five minutes longer between each subsequent visit.
- Unless your child seems ill or feels feverish, never make a great fuss over her. Don't get her out of bed to comfort her, or offer a drink of water, a toy or other diversion. Nighttime is sleepy time, not play time.
- Don't take her into your bed or allow her to crawl in with you. It's a hard habit to break once it starts. And what's more, you don't want to lose your privacy or the block of time away from her that you need every day.

What To Do If She Crawls Into Your Bed

Put her back firmly in her own bed, saying that she must sleep in her own bed. Tell her that if she lies in her bed quietly, you will come in and check on her in a few minutes. Keep your promise. If she remains awake, check on her again. If all else fails, you can lie down with her in her bed and then return to your own when she's asleep.

In Chapter 11, we talked about her limited understanding of object permanence in her first year. She doesn't have the sophistication to know that when you walk out of the room where she is, you haven't ceased to exist. When she hears you talking and moving about next door, she'll come to know that you aren't going to vanish. But even if she understands that you still exist when you are out of sight, she would still rather be right next to you and follow you into the other room. If she can't, she will probably howl in protest.

TIP: If your child shows this type of anxiety, give her extra love and snuggle time. Physical closeness will reassure her and give her the courage to sally forth on new expeditions. Don't leave her in a room alone until she feels more confident about separation from you. As we have mentioned, she is frightened of her new power to leave you. To help her feel comfortable with her new skill and calm her fear, play games with her which dramatize both situations.

Going Down the Drain

THE BATHTUB

One day your child loves to splash and play in her bath. Then, suddenly, she refuses to go near the bathtub when the water is running. She throws a tantrum when you draw her a bath and attempt to undress her in the bathroom. Or she may protest when the time comes to put her in the tub. As you lift her up, she arches her back and becomes rigid in defiance.

Why does she have this sudden shift in attitude? The answer is that she probably has had an opportunity to watch the water swirl and gurgle down the drain. If she was in the tub when the water drained out, her fear is probably more intense. But even standing next to the tub while it empties can be frightening. She reasons, "If the water can go down, I can go down too."

It doesn't usually help to reassure her that she is too big to go through that little hole. She's too little to understand the relationship of size to cause and effect. You will have more success if you let her play around water in nonthreatening ways, in places other than the bathroom. Let her wash a few unbreakable dishes or give her dolly a bath in the kitchen sink. She can fill the basin and then let the water out. She'll learn that her dolly can't go down the drain and finally make the connection that she herself can't go down either.

When she needs a bath, coax her ever so gently into the tub. Give her toys and try to make it fun. But if she clearly hates and fears it, get the job done and get her out. During this period you should keep the number of baths she must have to a minimum.

THE TOILET

Watching a toilet flush can exacerbate your child's fear of going down the drain: Its noisy, dramatic suction makes a great show of sloshing water and, unlike its tamer cousin the bathtub, it actually swallows objects. Your child may refuse to sit over the big hole of the toilet, or run away when it is flushed. What's more, she may resent that it takes away her bowel movement which she may not be ready to part with.

All in all, the toilet is usually far less satisfactory for toilet training than is the potty. Your child can manage getting on and off the potty herself; there's no climbing to do, no gaping watery hole to avoid. And because a potty usually resembles a child's chair, she will feel much more confident about using it on a regular basis.

Animism

HOUSEHOLD MONSTERS

Toilets, vacuum cleaners, lawn mowers and other household appliances can have the most remarkable effect on your child. She hears their noise, watches them move and becomes convinced that they are monsters. She is too little to know that they are not alive and dangerous. Her limited experience tells her she's in the middle of a real-life horror tale.

Let's take the vacuum cleaner as an example. At the flick of a switch a formerly docile, quiet beast begins to roar and move about the floor. Back and forth, back and forth it goes, edging nearer and nearer. Scary, isn't it? It would help, of of course, if she knew that it isn't a monster but simply an efficient means of cleaning the floor, and that it can't move on its own.

These inanimate monsters will continue to frighten your child until she understands their functions and that they are controllable machines. As she becomes more verbal and her understanding of the household routine increases, her fears will be eased somewhat. Even then it will be a long time before she feels comfortable when these machines are running.

TIPS: As long as her fear is intense, run the vacuum or mow the lawn when she isn't home, whenever possible. Buy her a toy sweeper and lawn mower to push around.

IMAGINARY BEASTS

As your child nears the end of her second year, you may find that invisible monsters have come to live in your house. They may rise up to haunt her especially when she goes to bed at night. She may show real fear (as distinguished from defiant refusal) when it is time to go to bed.

In an effort to calm her fears, you may find yourself shooing all the animals out of her room. Systematically, you move about the room, opening the closet door and looking under the bed. In a stern voice you order everybody out. Your child watches your ritual with a serious expression and, when you have finished, will give you a kiss and a hug and confidently settle in for the night.

Bodily Harm

Your child falls down and scrapes her knee. She cries and you comfort her. She looks down and sees blood oozing from her little cut and begins crying again. Why? Her limited experience hasn't taught her about the healing process; the concepts of blood clotting and a scab forming are totally unknown to her.

When she is bleeding, she doesn't understand what is happening. She fears that she's leaking and worries that her body is broken. She won't let up until you find a Band-Aid and cover the cut. Once the breach, however insignificant, has been successfully patched, and kissed better, she is reassured.

Her Guardian Angel

Your child has great confidence in you—as much as or more than you have in yourself. She strongly believes in your power to ward off the Bad Guys and keep her safe. You can help her get over many of her fears just by being there when she confronts them.

As her experience widens, the landscape of her anxieties and fears will change. You must be alert to the changes, watch over her progress, and step in when she falters. But try not to be overly protective. For just as you can't learn to walk for her, neither can you conquer her fears. In the end she is the one who must slay the dragons.

PART IV

TAKING CARE OF YOUR BABY'S HEALTH

No parent, however diligent, can catch all the hurts and discomforts of childhood before they happen. So you need to learn how to react appropriately—and quickly—to what has already occurred.

We are confident that you will find these chapters to be an indispensable part of your parenting library, but we must emphasize that they cannot possibly substitute for a first-aid class or lessons in cardio-pulmonary resuscitation (CPR) and other emergency procedures. Read further about each subject, using the bibliography provided, and take a course in first aid and CPR. Learn to utilize the services of the public safety agencies and consumer advocate groups. Tapping available sources will prepare you for whatever lies ahead.

Your innate common sense is the tool that will help you put your acquired knowledge to work. If, for example, your baby looks peaky and is unusually cranky, you will deduce that he may be ill and feel his forehead for fever.

Practical common sense has many applications. Its usefulness doesn't end with baby- and toddlerhood; it will go on being handy throughout the time you spend on the front line of parenting.

If you are feeling awed by the heavy responsibility of parenthood, don't be. Babies survive. They even thrive. Soon they grow older and, before you know it, they have grown up completely. Be comforted: You are already well along the road to success.

16

Health Matters

Y ou usually know right away when your child doesn't feel well. You can tell even without the obvious symptoms like vomiting or diarrhea. She may look flushed or peaked, feel warm or hot to your touch and may be crying, listless or cranky. She just isn't herself. What's worse, her illness may be interrupting her sleep.

When your baby or toddler is ill, it is important not to get flustered. Take her temperature (see below), note any significant symptoms and unusual behavior that seem to relate to her condition and call your pediatrician or family doctor. If you are concerned, don't hesitate or wait until later in the day to call. A fever by itself may not require an immediate call to your doctor, but when it is combined with irritability or pain, you should always call. When you get instructions from the doctor, follow them faithfully.

If illness comes in the middle of the night, you must use your judgment about waiting until morning to call. Any fever in a baby under six months old or, for those over six months old, a fever over 104 degrees Fahrenheit, especially if accompanied by severe pains or labored breathing, are examples of symptoms that can't wait until morning.

WELL-BABY CARE

Checkups for your new baby are crucial for her development. Her doctor needs to keep a running check on how she is growing physically and mentally and administer immunizations to protect her from disease (see below). She won't be permitted into school without written proof of immunization. And these visits may detect a medical condition that you as a lay person would be unable to notice.

The American Academy of Pediatrics (AAP) recommends a visit with your baby's physician at two, four, six, nine and 12 months. The AAP suggests visits at 18 and 24 months in the second year. Many pediatricians want to see their babies more frequently than the AAP requires.

IMMUNIZATION SCHEDULE

Vaccine	Age
DTP (diphtheria, tetanus and pertussis or whooping cough)	2 months
Polio	
DTP, Polio	4 months
DTP, Polio	6 months
MMR (measles, mumps and rubella)	15 months
DTP, Polio	18 months
DTP, Polio	4–5 years

Fever

Your child may or may not have a fever when she is sick. Noting the way she acts is just as important as taking her temperature. Babies often run high temperatures, sometimes for little or no apparent reason. Though there's no cause for undue alarm, you should alert your doctor.

One of the first habits you develop as a new parent is putting your hand on your baby's forehead to determine if you should get out the rectal thermometer. Another quick, more accurate way is to place a small tape digital thermometer, sometimes called a fever strip, on her forehead. You may want to confirm the reading with a rectal thermometer, but remember that rectal temps are about one degree higher.

FEBRILE CONVULSIONS

About 5 percent of all children from six months to the age of four or five have febrile convulsions when they have temperatures as high as 104 degrees. Often a child will convulse because there is a sudden rise to a 102- or 103-degree fever. The symptoms of these convulsions are frightening to parents: jerking limbs, eyes rolling back, paleness and unresponsiveness or even unconsciousness. They are seldom dangerous, however, and often stop spontaneously after a few minutes. If your child convulses, you should act quickly and calmly.

WHAT TO DO:

1. Lay her face down. *Never* lay her on her back.
2. Make sure she can breathe freely and has nothing in her mouth.
3. Sponge her with water.
4. Do not leave her unattended.
5. Call her doctor immediately.

MEASURING FEVER

A rectal thermometer is often recommended for taking your baby's or toddler's temperature. A rectal temperature is usually one degree *higher* than a mouth temperature. Alternate ways of measuring fever are under the arm and by a digital tape placed on the child's forehead. Because an oral thermometer is made of glass and mercury and might break in their mouths, small babies and children should *never* have their temperature taken orally. You should use the method your doctor recommends.

Using a rectal thermometer:

1. Disinfect the thermometer by dipping it into rubbing alcohol. (You can't use hot water for obvious reasons.)
2. Rinse it thoroughly in cold water.
3. Shake it repeatedly to bring the mercury below 97 degrees.
4. Lubricate the tip with petroleum jelly.
5. Lay your baby or toddler over your knees, spread her buttocks with your fingers, and gently insert the silver-tipped end one inch into her rectum.
6. Hold it in place for two to three minutes.

SAFETY TIP: Your child is likely to protest this procedure quite vehemently. She may squirm and try to escape. To hold her down firmly, you may have to enlist help. After inserting the thermometer, use the following method when holding it in place:

Open your hand and place it on her bottom with the thermometer between your fingers. You can safely ride out the storm of protest without danger of jabbing her or breaking the thermometer. Speak calmly to her. Tell her that you are trying to help her feel better. Keep your mind on what you are doing and don't let her protests upset you.

Getting Well Quickly

1. Encourage rest. If your child is sick and wants to sleep, let her sleep. Keep the room darkened and quiet to encourage her to rest. Don't worry about her schedule. Extra rest will help her body heal and you'll both get a break from crankiness, crying or other expressions of discomfort.
2. Unless she has been vomiting, offer her clear liquids like broth (remember Grandma's chicken soup?), carbonated beverages and water. Loss of appetite is normal when a child doesn't feel well.
3. Provide extra comfort measures. Cuddle her more. Your tenderness and love are wonderful medicine for her.
4. Be calm when carrying out the doctor's instructions. Do what needs to be done without fuss and fanfare. Your matter-of-fact attitude will be communicated to your child and her fears will diminish.

GIVING MEDICINE

Medicine for your baby or toddler comes in a liquid form. While it is easy for your child to swallow, your job—getting it into her mouth—isn't always so easy. She may protest the medicine's taste and spit it out. Using a spoon without spilling its contents is often a challenge.

Use an eye dropper for baby medicine. If you give your baby vitamins, you are already familiar with the technique: Hold your baby in your arms with her head elevated slightly. Measure the exact dosage and gently insert the dropper into her mouth.

When your baby nears toddlerhood and prescribed doses are larger than one dropper can hold, you can use a plastic vial with a wide scoop-like mouth. Use the hash marks on the vial to measure the desired dosage, hold your child as before and tip it into her mouth.

Common Complaints

During your child's first two years you will need to be on the alert for a long list of medical conditions. Most of these aren't serious and all of them can be treated effectively or will disappear on their own without treatment. There is no way, of course, to predict which complaints your child will have, so you should be aware of all ailments that are common in babies and toddlers.

The list that follows identifies and describes them briefly and discusses how they can be handled effectively. We shall begin with the eye, ear, nose and throat and move south to the respiratory, digestive and urinary tracts. As you read, you can take comfort from the fact that you will never have to handle them all!

WARNING: You must never diagnose or medicate your child without consulting her pediatrician or family doctor. It is important to follow their advice carefully. The procedures below are in no way intended to replace that advice: Our list is for information only.

EYES

Conjunctivitis (also known as pink eye and sticky eye): An infection of the outer lining of the eyeball and lid caused by a virus, bacteria or a piece of dirt. The eye is sometimes itchy and may have a yellowish discharge.

WHAT MAY HELP: Swab away discharge with a moistened sterile cotton ball. Wash out any grit from the eye. Your doctor may prescribe antibiotic drops. We suggest you get someone to help you hold your child if you need to put antibiotics in her eye.

To administer drops: Tilt back your child's head and put the drops on the outer edge of her eye. As she blinks, the drops will seep in.

Sty: An infected pimple or boil on the outer edge of the eyelid near the eyelash which will heal in a few days.

WHAT MAY HELP: Warm cotton compresses every three to four hours until the sty comes to a head. Do not try to pop it. Your doctor will probably prescribe an antibiotic. (See procedure to administer antibiotic under *Conjunctivitis,* above.)

Squint (also known as cross-eyed): Eyes looking in different directions at the same time. In a newborn the condition may disappear as she gains control of her eyes. A persistent squint may mean impaired vision.

WHAT MAY HELP: If the condition persists, an ophthalmologist (eye specialist) or a pediatric ophthalmologist should be consulted. Treatment depends upon the cause of the problem. Glasses or an eye patch are often recommended.

EAR, NOSE AND THROAT

The ear, nose and throat are connected and infections can, and often do, move around freely. In addition, symptoms frequently appear in more than one organ simultaneously.

Earaches *(otitis externa):* An infection in the outer ear causing either pain or itchiness.

WHAT MAY HELP: If a doctor determines this is not a middle ear infection, he may prescribe drops and advise you to keep the ear canal dry until it clears up.

Ear infections *(otitis media):* As the Latin name suggests, an ear infection affects the middle ear. It is easily the most common and painful of children's ailments. There is usually a lot of pain associated with it. A young baby or toddler will often rub or pull her ear. She may be feverish or complain of a headache. She may cry a lot, especially at night, when pressure builds up and pain intensifies. In addition, she may be temporarily deaf because of excess fluid buildup.

WHAT MAY HELP: Acetaminophen may be prescribed to lower fever and relieve pain, and decongestants to drain the infected area. Frequent occurrences may lead to a consultation with an ear, nose and throat specialist, who in turn may recommend surgical insertion of tiny plastic myringotomy tubes to aid drainage in the ears. Many experts think that these tubes ventilate and help to heal the lining of the middle ear.

Allergic rhinitis (better known as hay fever or chronic stuffy nose): Blocked nasal passages are sometimes accompanied by watering eyes and sneezing. Rhinitis is a sign of an allergic reaction in the nasal passages caused by pollen, house dust or some other substance.

WHAT MAY HELP: Nose drops, sprays and antihistamines may be prescribed, depending on your child's age and the severity of the condition. If your child always has a stuffy nose or has severe seasonal bouts with it, you may want to consult an allergist to try to determine the source of the allergy.

The common cold: A viral infection of the nose and throat which has no known cure other than the passage of time. A runny nose or stuffy nose, a fever, sore throat and cough are typical cold symptoms. Newborn babies with blocked air passages have trouble breathing through their mouths. Breathing is still a new exercise to them, and if they get a cold, they need extra help.

WHAT MAY HELP: Your doctor may prescribe nose drops and a small dose of acetaminophen for your newborn and suggest that she sleep with her head elevated. Because you can't put a pillow in the crib, you may find her sleeping in your arms. Acetaminophen may relieve an older baby's or toddler's fever and sore throat.

Pharyngitis and sore throat: An inflammation of the pharynx and the walls of the throat which may be accompanied by fever, a cough and a runny nose. Occasionally there can be a bacterial infection and it can turn into *strep throat,* which is caused by streptococcus bacteria. If a strep throat is not treated, your child is at risk for rheumatic fever or a throat abscess.

WHAT MAY HELP: Acetaminophen will relieve pain and fever. The physician may take a culture from your child's throat with a cotton swab and run a test to determine if strep is present. If it is, an antibiotic will be prescribed.

Tonsillitis: A viral inflammation of the tonsils, a pair of glands lying on either side of the back of the throat. Symptoms are a sore throat, fever, loss of appetite, swollen glands under the chin and around the neck. The condition usually lasts three or four days.

WHAT MAY HELP: Acetaminophen will relieve pain and fever and antibiotics may be prescribed. In earlier times tonsils were routinely removed in an operation called a tonsillectomy. Today the operation is less frequently performed, reserved only for those children who have recurrent attacks of tonsillitis.

Laryngitis and croup: *Laryngitis* is an inflammation of the larynx (also known as the voice box), resulting in loss of voice. *Croup* is an infection in the tissues around the larynx, which causes a loud, barking cough, fever and noisy breathing. The harshness of the cough can frighten parents and the child herself, but it needn't be a cause for alarm.

WHAT MAY HELP: Laryngitis will probably disappear on its own after a few days. For croup, the air of a cold steam vaporizer may soothe coughing and acetaminophen will relieve any fever. Whenever a child has croup she should always be examined by a doctor.

Nosebleeds: Spontaneous nosebleeds are fairly common in toddlers and older children and are an indication of infection in the lining of the nose. They are alarming to both parents and the child, but are rarely dangerous or serious. NOTE: If your child is prone to nosebleeds, never go *anywhere* without tissues.

WHAT MAY HELP: The bleeding may be controlled by pinching the nostrils with a cold washcloth and applying pressure for a few minutes until a clot can form. Your child should be sitting up and leaning forward in order to keep the blood from running down her throat. If she has frequent nosebleeds, consult her doctor.

THE MOUTH AND TEETH

Teething: Though it is a normal and necessary aspect of growing up and is not an illness, teething can be very painful. While cutting new teeth doesn't seem to bother some babies, for others it is a very uncomfortable process. Whether she has discomfort or not, your baby will be drooling long before the tooth actually appears. If teething bothers her, she'll be cranky and have trouble sleeping.

WHAT MAY HELP: You'll find that she will bite on everything she can. Offer her smooth hard rattles, hard breads and teething biscuits to gnaw on. Some so-called teethers are available that can be put into the refrigerator before use. The coldness feels good on sore gums. In addition, there are over-the-counter topical remedies that are suitable for young babies.

Mouth infections (also known as thrush): Thrush is a common yeast infection in babies which produces white patches on the tongue, gums or inside of the cheek. Though this type of infection is not serious, it can make drinking from a bottle or nursing quite painful for a baby.

WHAT MAY HELP: The pediatrician may prescribe antifungal drops. More careful sterilization of bottles may prevent a recurrence of the condition.

Mouth ulcers: These are viral infections which usually disappear on their own.

WHAT MAY HELP: Treatment is not usually necessary. An antiseptic cream prescribed by the doctor may soothe pain if needed.

THE LUNGS

WARNING: Never smoke in the same room with a child who has an acute or chronic respiratory illness.

Asthma or wheezing: The shrinking of the small breathing tubes (bronchioles) in the lungs, caused by an allergic reaction to pollen, animal fur, feathers or house dust. A viral lung infection can trigger the condition as well. It is relatively common in children and usually occurs in families with a history of allergic reactions. Your child may grow out of asthma and have normal lungs later in life.

WHAT MAY HELP: There are several drugs which can be taken orally or inhaled from an aerosol that will dilate the bronchioles. If the condition is persistent or serious, an allergist can be consulted to determine the cause of the allergic reaction.

Bronchiolitis: A viral infection of the small air tubes in the lungs, a cousin of the common cold. This condition may start with a runny nose and sneezing and then settle into the lungs; your baby may develop a cough and a wheeze or have difficulty breathing.

WHAT MAY HELP: There is no cure other than time, though your doctor may prescribe an antibiotic to ward off a secondary infection. Any problems that develop over sleeping, eating or breathing should be brought immediately to your physician's attention.

Bronchitis: A viral infection in the large breathing tubes in the lungs, similar to bronchiolitis. The coughing may be more severe than when the small tubes are infected. The condition usually disappears within a week and does no permanent damage.

WHAT MAY HELP: The baby's physician may prescribe a soothing cough mixture and, if indicated, an anti-wheeze drug. Plenty of liquids will help flush out the virus. As with bronchiolitis, an antibiotic may be prescribed.

Pneumonia: A bacterial or viral infection of the small air sacs or alveoli, located at the end of the breathing tubes in the lungs. Symptoms are a cough and fever and the patient will feel very ill. Your doctor can detect pneumonia by listening to your child's chest and may want to confirm it with a chest X-ray at the hospital.

WHAT MAY HELP: Acetaminophen may be used to reduce fever, and an antibiotic will be prescribed, if it is a bacterial infection or to prevent a secondary infection.

THE DIGESTIVE TRACT

Abdominal pain, or stomachache: A tummyache can have many causes, most of which are not serious. It can accompany a cold because the abdominal lymph glands have enlarged. It can accompany other symptoms such as vomiting, diarrhea or constipation caused by an infection or obstruction in the bowel (see *Gastroenteritis* below), or it can be connected to the frequent urination that results from a *urinary tract infection* (see below).

WARNING: Any persistent or severe pain should be brought to your pediatrician's attention.

Appendicitis is an inflammation of the appendix, a small sac attached to the bowel, which often starts with pain in the center of the abdomen. The pain increases and moves to the lower right side. When appendicitis is diagnosed, a surgical procedure to remove the appendix is usually suggested.

WHAT MAY HELP: A mild stomachache can sometimes be relieved by drawing the knees up or by stretching out. Trial and error will help determine which position might help.

Constipation: Hard stools that are difficult to expel—and which may be streaked with blood from tiny tears in the tissue around the anus—indicate that your child is constipated. How often a stool is passed varies naturally from child to child and the length of the interval between bowel movements does not by itself indicate constipation. If your child's stools are soft or firm and she can pass them without straining, she is not constipated.

WHAT MAY HELP: Consult your pediatrician at once, because a change in diet can usually cure the problem. For a baby your doctor may suggest extra water or a little diluted prune juice. An older child should eat a varied diet that includes fiber-rich whole grain cereals and plenty of fruits and vegetables.

Diarrhea: Frequent bowel movements that are loose may either be a reaction to a certain food or could indicate an infection in the bowel (see *Gastroenteritis* below). The greatest concern with diarrhea is dehydration, which can occur if body fluids are not replaced quickly enough.

WHAT MAY HELP: An increase of fluids is vital. Depending on the cause of the diarrhea, your doctor may order either a temporary or a permanent change in your child's diet.

Gastroenteritis: The medical term for diarrhea caused by a bacterial or viral infection of the bowel. Symptoms include diarrhea, a stomachache and fever. Dehydration resulting from loss of body fluids is a complication to be avoided. The condition usually disappears after a few days.

WHAT MAY HELP: Offer your child a clear liquid diet: flat ginger ale, weak tea, clear soup. If she is still a baby, your doctor may suggest one of the over-the-counter "ideal clear liquids" which will replenish her essential minerals. Phone your doctor once a day as long as she is on a clear liquid diet.

Vomiting: Your child may vomit as a reaction to infection or because of an obstruction in the bowel. This is not to be confused with a baby's spitting up or regurgitating a small amount of milk after a feeding. If your child vomits and also has other symptoms such as stomachache, diarrhea, headache or feeding difficulties, you should alert your doctor.

WHAT MAY HELP: Take your child off solid food and offer her one teaspoon of clear liquid or flat Coke every half hour until vomiting stops. When it has stopped, offer one to two ounces of clear liquid maximum every hour. If your child has been vomiting for four to six hours, call your doctor.

URINARY TRACT

Urinary infections: A bacterial infection of all or part of the tract, which includes the kidneys, the ureters, the bladder and urethra. There can be many symptoms: painful or frequent urination, abdominal pain, blood in the urine, fever, fluid retention, vomiting and loss of appetite. An infection is detected by testing a urine sample and proper treatment is required in order to avoid damage to the kidneys.

WHAT MAY HELP: The condition can be cured by an antibiotic prescribed by your child's pediatrician and plenty of fluids to wash out the infection. A follow-up urine test will be needed to determine that the infection has completely gone.

SKIN RASHES

Diaper rash: A red blotchy rash on your baby's bottom is either a reaction to being wet and soiled or the result of a fungal infection.

WHAT MAY HELP: Give your baby air baths, change her diaper more frequently and apply a barrier cream. If a fungus is present, an antifungal cream will be prescribed.

Eczema: Red and itchy skin which spreads over the baby's face and body. As a child gets older, eczema usually concentrates in the areas around the elbow, knee, wrist and ankle.

WHAT MAY HELP: Tight-fitting, rough-textured clothes should be avoided in favor of loose, all-cotton garments that allow the skin to breathe. Your physician may prescribe an oil or ointment for the affected area.

Prickly Heat: A red, almost pimply rash around your child's face, neck and bottom caused by blocked sweat glands.

WHAT MAY HELP: The rash will disappear in a few days without treatment. In hot weather, keep your child cool to prevent the rash from recurring.

GENERAL CONDITIONS

Colic: Nobody really knows what causes a young baby's recurring bouts of nonstop crying and discomfort, which can happen at any time of the day or night, but are especially common in the late afternoon and early evening. There are many theories, but no proof. Babies often feel better when sucking and may be overeating and/or swallowing a lot of air as a result.

If your baby is colicky, she may draw her legs up as if in abdominal pain; consoling her will be difficult. Be sure to have your doctor examine her to make certain there isn't another cause of her unhappiness. Happily, colic is a temporary condition and rarely lasts beyond the baby's third month.

WHAT MAY HELP: Coping with colic is often a function of trial and error. Do what you can to prevent the long bouts of crying which cause her to swallow even more air. Here are some techniques to try:

1. Try sitting with her lying face down over your knees. This works either because the pressure on her abdomen relieves the pain or because the novel view may distract her.
2. Walk, carrying her upright over your shoulder, and rub her back gently.
3. Take her for a ride in the car.
4. Reduce her formula to 32 to 36 ounces a day and spend plenty of time burping her.

Motion or Travel Sickness: Some children feel sick when they travel and may vomit when riding in cars, buses, boats, trains and planes.

WHAT MAY HELP: Fresh air and an unobstructed view of the scenery or horizon as it passes by will help your child. Because milk may cause her to vomit, you may want to avoid giving her any, either just before you leave or while you are in transit. Consult your doctor regarding any medication for motion sickness.

You Can't Ask a Stupid Question

Choosing a family doctor or pediatrician in whom you can feel complete trust is the linchpin of your child's well-being. Having confidence in the doctor you select and the medical advice he or she gives you is crucial for your peace of mind.

In addition to advising you when your child is ill, most pediatricians also have calling hours to handle the routine—but important—questions that don't require an office visit. Take advantage of the medical expertise they offer at no extra charge.

Never hesitate to ask. *No* question is stupid if you don't know the answer.

17

First Aid and Emergency Situations

As the saying goes, "Accidents happen" and it is important to know how to react and treat your child when they do. You can learn how to handle nearly any situation by taking courses in first-aid treatment and cardio-pulmonary resuscitation (CPR). We strongly recommend that you do both. Knowing the right treatment assures your child of proper care when he needs it and it also reassures you when you are concerned about his safety.

What follows first is a list of common nonemergency first-aid situations along with general tips about what to do and what not to do, and also how to tell when your child needs medical attention. A listing of more serious situations—and full-fledged emergencies—begins on page 205.

Wounds

Animal Bites: Check with your doctor to see if your child needs a tetanus booster. A superficial bite can be cleaned with warm water and covered with a sterile gauze dressing. More serious bites such as those on the face or neck and, *because of the* *danger of rabies, any bite from an unknown animal,* all require immediate medical attention.

Insect Bites: Mosquito, flea and chigger bites are itchy and can be soothed with calamine lotion. Cover the bite to prevent your child from scratching it.

Bee and wasp stings are painful. If you can see the stinger sticking up, pull it out with tweezers. Don't try to squeeze it out. Soak a piece of cotton in a paste of meat tenderizer, bicarbonate of soda or Epsom salts and apply to the sting. If your child has been stung several times at once, give him a bath laced with Epsom salts. If there is marked swelling, head-to-toe hives, troubled breathing or swallowing, which signal an allergic reaction, call your doctor immediately and watch for signs of shock (see *Signs of Shock* box on page 208).

Blisters: Skin rubbed raw by friction or by a burn develops a natural bubble-like protection to cover the damaged skin surface. Cover it with gauze to allow the blister to rise and fall on its own. Don't prick it. If it bursts early, keep it clean and dry.

Cuts and Scratches: Minor wounds can be treated at home. Clean them with warm water, using a sterile gauze swab. Pat dry and apply a mild antiseptic. Cover with a gauze adhesive. Deep wounds and those that are bleeding profusely need medical attention (see *Bleeding* on page 208).

Splinter: All splinters need to be removed; splinters left in place can become infected and very sore. Never attempt to extract glass or metal from your child's skin. Seek medical help.

PROCEDURE FOR EXTRACTION: To loosen the splinter, soak the area in a solution of Epsom salts or bicarbonate of soda. Sterilize a needle with antiseptic and rinse. Gently probe the immediate area around the object to further loosen it from its niche. Continue until you have cleared away the surrounding tissue and exposed it enough for tweezers to get hold of it. Extract the splinter with tweezers, then apply antiseptic and a gauze adhesive.

Specific Injuries

Crushed fingers: Slamming doors and drawers are painful traps for exploring fingers. If your child gets his fingers caught, first make sure he can move them. If he can't, if there is any damage to the fingers, or if the pain doesn't subside, call your doctor. A cold compress will help reduce the pain and swelling and a bandage will protect it.

Eye injuries: If your child has had any injury to his eye, tape a gauze eye patch over his eye and seek medical attention immediately.

Head injuries: Bangs on the head are common in early childhood and are usually not serious unless your child loses consciousness, vomits, seems drowsy or has a severe headache. Any of the above should signal that medical help is needed.

Mouth injuries: If your child has cut his tongue, lip or cheek, even the smallest wounds will bleed profusely and you may find this hard to stop. If he has bitten through his tongue or lip, give him an ice cube wrapped in cloth and call your doctor. Mouth injuries heal fast and seldom require stitches. A liquid or soft diet may be required for a while, though.

Sprains: A sprain is an injury to the soft tissue around a joint. An ankle, finger, wrist and knee are most likely to be sprained. Signs of a sprain are pain, swelling and tenderness to the touch. A cold compress will help both pain and swelling. So will rest and elevating the sprained area. If feasible, wrap the area lightly in an elastic bandage (during the day only, not during the night). If the pain and swelling don't go away after several days, consult your doctor.

Presence of Foreign Bodies

In the eye: Grit and dirt can be washed out with water. Larger or more stubborn matter can be removed with the tip of a handkerchief or tissue. *Don't let your child rub his eye because it will irritate and possibly damage the eye further.* A gauze bandage over his eye will help keep his hands away.

In the ear: Don't try to remove it either by flushing it out or forcibly extracting it. Seek medical help.

In the nose: Some children stick small items up their noses. An unpleasant discharge is a sign that a child has done so. If possible, see if he can dislodge it by blowing his nose. If he can't, you'll need a medical expert.

Swallowed objects: As we discussed in earlier chapters, young babies put everything in their mouths, including things they shouldn't eat. If your child has swallowed something that will probably pass through his system without harming him, watch his diaper for the item he ate. If necessary, probe each bowel movement to make sure the item passes. If the foreign body doesn't travel as far as the stomach, he will feel pain, may drool from the mouth and could have difficulty breathing.

- If someone is with you, one of you should call for help while the other is applying first aid.
- If you are alone, first aid comes first.
- A serious accident requires an ambulance, particularly if you shouldn't move your child.
- Drowsiness, vomiting, unconsciousness, bleeding from ears or nose or heavy blood loss after an accident are signs that you should take your child to the hospital emergency room.
- In many situations you can phone your doctor and arrange to meet at his or her office or a nearby hospital emergency room.
- If you are on vacation, go straight to the nearest hospital emergency room.
- Watch for signs of shock (see box on page 208).

SAFETY TIP: Post important emergency phone numbers of your local fire and police departments, ambulance service and poison control center on every telephone in the house. If your phones have speed dial capability, program them as automatic numbers so they can be dialed at the push of a button.

Some things, like tiny watch batteries and sharp objects, are causes for real concern. If you have reason to believe your baby has swallowed something dangerous, seek medical help immediately. Another hazard of swallowed objects is choking (see *Choking* on page 209).

Important Miscellany

Overheating and Heatstroke: Signs of heatstroke are flushed complexion, restlessness, a raised temperature and general malaise. Undress your child and sponge him with cool water; offer him sips of cool, not iced water. Seek medical help.

Sunburn: If your child gets sunburned, a cool bath and calamine lotion will soothe the pain.

Frostbite: When exposed to extreme cold, skin becomes red at first, then changes to gray or white. When the skin is thawing, blisters may form on skin that has been frostbitten. Apply warm compresses to a white area until the skin reddens. Separate fingers or toes with a clean, dry cloth.
Contact your doctor immediately.

EMERGENCIES: A TO Z

Though we hope it won't ever happen to you, emergencies *can* arise and you'll need to act fast. It is important to familiarize yourself with the procedures that will help your child. Below is a list of situations that need important first-aid measures while you are waiting for medical attention.

Cardio-Pulmonary Resuscitation

If your child isn't breathing and his heart has stopped beating, administer CPR immediately, even if you fear it may be too late.

ARTIFICIAL RESPIRATION

1. Lay the child on his back. Clear his mouth with your finger of blood, vomit or objects.
2. Tilt his head gently back and lift the chin up and forward so his tongue isn't blocking his throat.
3. Pinch his nostrils and seal your mouth over his open mouth.

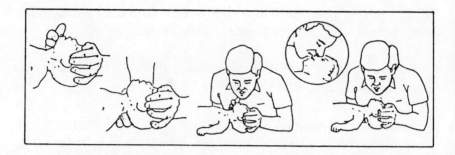

4. Give one breath every three seconds (a little faster for a baby). Continue until the baby or child begins breathing on his own, or until help arrives.
5. When breathing is restored, gently roll him over to the recovery position (see page 207).

NOTE: For babies and young toddlers you can put your mouth over both mouth and nose. Give four quick breaths, checking that the chest rises and falls.

HEART MASSAGE

If, after some effort with artificial respiration, your child is very pale or a blue-gray color, his heart may have stopped.

1. Check the carotid pulse (below the jaw in line with the ear).
2. If no pulse is felt, alternate massaging his heart with artificial respiration. After five heart compressions, return to artificial respiration for one breath.

NOTE: If you have someone with you, one can respirate him while the other massages the heart.

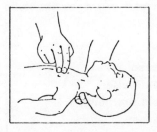

For a child under two: Use two fingers and press gently down on lower breastbone at a rate of about 100 times per minute.

For a child over two: Use the heel of your palm and press more firmly 60 to 80 times per minute.

RECOVERY POSITION

If your child is unconscious, it is important to lay him on his stomach to prevent the throat from being blocked by the tongue, blood or vomit. If he is breathing, but drowsy or unconscious and he is lying on his back, you need to turn him over *gently:*

1. Kneel down and turn his head toward you.
2. Place his hand nearest you under his bottom, palm up.
3. Place the other arm across his chest.
4. Bend the leg on the far side and draw it over the leg closest to you.
5. Place your hand under his head and roll him over toward you onto his stomach.
6. His final position: The arm and leg nearest you are bent, his head is turned to face you.

SIGNS OF SHOCK

Paleness	Nausea
Sweating	Rapid pulse
General unwell condition	Rapid breathing
Faintness	Delirium

What To Do:

1. Lay your child down with his head turned to the side.
2. Loosen his clothing.
3. Raise his legs.
4. Cover him with a blanket.
5. If he loses consciousness, put him in the *recovery position* (see drawing on previous page) and call for immediate help.

Specific Emergency Situations

BLEEDING

Major loss of blood must be controlled quickly:

1. Apply pressure to the wound using a clean cloth or your hand.
2. Elevate the wound.
3. Keep your child still.
4. Watch for shock (see box above).

If a bone is protruding or a sharp object is sticking in the wound:

Press around the wound.
Don't remove the object.

BURNS

1. Immerse burned area in cold water for ten minutes or longer.
2. Remove tight-fitting clothing.
    NOTE: If clothes are stuck to skin, do *not* try to remove them.
3. Take care not to burst any blisters.
4. *Minor* burns should be covered with gauze or cloth to prevent infection.

Clothes on fire:

1. Use water, if readily available, to douse the child.
    or
2. Get him on the ground and smother flames with a non-synthetic rug, blanket, towel or coat.
3. If none of the above is available, you can use your own body to cover his. Make sure there is no air gap between you.

CHOKING

For a baby:

- Hold him face down over your arm or hold him up side down by his legs.
- Give him four sharp slaps with an open hand in between his shoulder blades.

For a child:

- Sit with crossed legs and lay him face down over your knees with his head down.
- Give him four sharp slaps with an open hand in between his shoulder blades.

Once he has expelled the object he choked on, you can scoop it out of his mouth with your finger before turning him right side up. *Do not* try to scoop out something deeply lodged as it may just wedge itself even deeper into his throat.

The Heimlich Maneuver
(If slapping him while he is upside down doesn't work):

- Stand or sit and face your child away from you.
- Use two fingers on both of your hands and give four sharp thrusts to the center upper abdomen (between navel and breastbone) to force air out and dislodge the object.

DROWNING

1. Get the child out of the water.
2. Empty his mouth.
3. If breathing has stopped, administer CPR. (He'll cough up water when breathing returns.)
4. Send for an ambulance.

ELECTRIC SHOCK

1. *Never* touch a child who has made any electrical contact.
2. Take extra care if water is around, as it conducts electricity.
3. Break the electric current by doing the following:
   (a) Turn off the main switch or fuse box.
   (b) Pull the plug.
   (c) Using a nonconducting object made of wood or plastic (a broom or a chair, for example), push the child away from the wire or outlet.
4. Check his breathing and administer CPR, if necessary. He may need treatment for burns or shock as well.

FRACTURES

If you have reason to believe your child has broken a limb or clavicle (collarbone), don't move him unless you have to in order to get medical assistance. This is especially important if his neck or back may be injured as well.

1. Immobilize the limb.
2. Watch for signs of shock (see box on page 208).

Leg:

1. Place rolled or folded padding between legs.
2. Tie legs together at knees and feet using triangles (or folded squares) of cloth.

Arm: To make a sling:

1. Place a triangle (or folded square) of cloth on his chest with one corner near his head.
2. Gently bend the injured arm across his chest.
3. Fold the cloth over his arm and bring the third corner up.
4. Tie the two corners around his neck.

POISONING

If you suspect your child has swallowed a poisonous substance, try to determine what it is.

HOW TO INDUCE VOMITING

- For a child over one year old, give one tablespoon of Syrup of Ipecac plus at least one cup of water.
- If no ipecac is available or the child is under a year old, tickle the back of his throat with a blunt object like a spoon handle.
- Hold the child's head upright as he vomits.

If you know what he swallowed:

1. Read the label and follow instructions.
2. If there is no label, call a Poison Control Center and/or your doctor.

or

3. Call a rescue unit or take your child to the nearest hospital emergency room. Bring along the unswallowed remains or the container it came in.

If you don't know what he swallowed:

1. *Never* try an antidote you think *might* work. What helps some poisons can aggravate others.
2. Drive immediately to the nearest hospital emergency room.

NOTE: Induce vomiting only if you are directed to.

Appendix A

Tracking Your Baby's Development

The charts that follow show how boy and girl babies increase their length (or height, as we think of it once they start standing up) and weight at six-monthly intervals from birth to two years old. The shaded areas at the top of the bars show the wide range of variation that can be expected at each stage. You may want to fill in your own baby's record at the side of each chart. The charts are based on information from the National Center for Health Statistics and drawn by Dana Burns.

Milestones in Your Baby's Development shows the approximate age in months at which various percentages of all children commonly achieve specific skills. It is taken from a useful and informative newsletter, *Growing Child,* which is available through your pediatrician or by subscription from Dunn & Hargitt, Inc., 22 North 2nd Street, Lafayette, IN 47902.

LENGTHS FOR BOY AND GIRL BABIES
FROM BIRTH TO 24 MONTHS

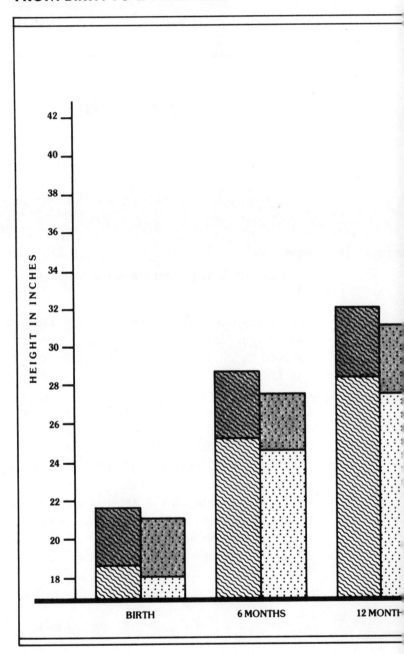

BOYS

GILRS

8 MONTHS   24 MONTHS

YOUR BABY'S RECORD

BIRTH _____

6 MONTHS _____

12 MONTHS _____

18 MONTHS _____

24 MONTHS _____

WEIGHTS FOR BOY AND GIRL BABIES
FROM BIRTH TO 24 MONTHS

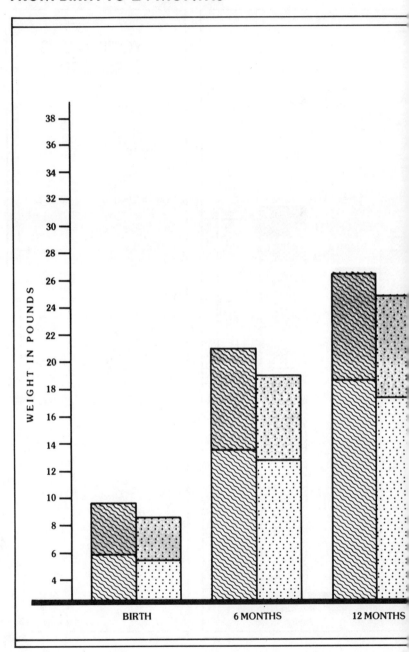

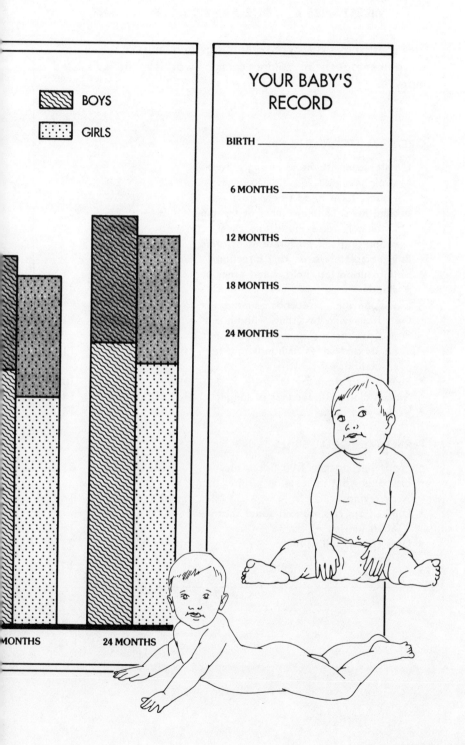

BOYS

GIRLS

MONTHS 24 MONTHS

YOUR BABY'S RECORD

BIRTH _____

6 MONTHS _____

12 MONTHS _____

18 MONTHS _____

24 MONTHS _____

MILESTONES IN YOUR BABY'S DEVELOPMENT

This chart shows the approximate age in months at which various percentages of all children commonly achieve the skills listed here.

	50%	75%	90%
GROSS MOTOR SKILLS			
• On stomach, lifts head strongly, face straight ahead	2	2½	3½
• On back, turns head freely from side to side, head centered most of the time	2	2½	3
• On stomach, raises head and chest, supporting self on forearms or arms	3	3½	4½
• Rolls completely over, any direction	2½	3½	4½
• Sitting supported, holds head erect and steady	3	3½	4½
• Sits alone for 30 seconds or more	6	7	9
• Gets from lying to sitting without aid	8	9½	11
• Prewalking progression, creeping on hands and knees or hands and feet; sit-and-hitch	7	10	11
• Pulls self to stand by furniture	7	9	10
• Stands alone, 10 seconds or longer	10½	13	14
• Walks well alone	12	13½	14
PERSONAL SOCIAL SKILLS			
• Feeds self cracker, fruit tidbit, etc.	5½	6½	8
• Indicates want in some way other than by crying	12	13½	14
• Drinks from cup without spout that he holds himself	11½	14	16
• Uses spoon, spills little	14½	18	24

	50%	75%	90%
FINE MOTOR SKILLS			
• Picks up small object (crumb, raisin) between tips of forefinger and thumb	10½	12½	14½
• Scribbles spontaneously with crayon, pencil, etc.	13½	16	24
LANGUAGE SKILLS			
• Says 3 words other than "mama" and "dada"	13	15	21

SOURCE: *Growing Child,* © 1980.

Appendix B

How Do You Interact with Your Child?

These charts have been designed for you to record how your toddler behaves and what your reactions are, so that you will be able to analyze your interactions as we suggested in Chapter 14. As your goal in a project like this is to look for patterns, the charts have space for four days' worth of notes, which should allow you to form an idea of the types of behaviors that are involved. If you need additional charts or space, we suggest that you take copies.

TYPE OF BEHAVIOR	ISSUE/SITUATION	WHEN
DAY ONE		
DAY TWO		

INTERACTION CHARTS

WHERE	MY RESPONSES	WHAT HAPPENED NEXT

TYPE OF BEHAVIOR	ISSUE/SITUATION	WHEN
DAY THREE		
DAY FOUR		

INTERACTION CHARTS

WHERE	MY RESPONSES	WHAT HAPPENED NEXT

Bibliography

SPECIFICALLY FOR FATHERS

Between Father and Child: How to Become the Kind of Father You Want to Be, by Ronald H. Levant and John Kelly (New York: Viking, 1989).

Confessions of a Pregnant Father, by Dan Greenburg (New York: Macmillan, 1986).

Daddy: The Diary of an Expectant Father, by Dennis Denziger (Tucson, AZ: HP Books, 1987).

Daughters and Fathers, edited by Lynda E. Boose and Betty S. Flowers (Baltimore: Johns Hopkins University Press, 1989)

Dimensions of Fatherhood, by Shirley M. Hanson and Frederick W. Bozett (Beverly Hills, CA: Sage, 1985).

Father and Child: Developmental and Clinical Perspectives, by S. Cath, A. Gurwitt and J. Ross (Boston: Little, Brown, 1982).

Fatherhood, by Bill Cosby (Garden City, NY: Doubleday, 1986).

Fatherhood U.S.A.: The First National Guide to Programs, Services and Resources for and about Fathers, by Debra Klinman and Rhiana Kohl (New York: Garland, 1984).

Fathering, by Maureen Green (New York: McGraw-Hill, 1976).

Fathering, by C. Phillips and J. Anzalone (St. Louis: C.V. Mosby, 1978).

Fathers and Their Families, edited by S. Cath, A. Gurwitt and L. Gunsberg (Hillsdale, NJ: Analytic Press, 1989).

The Expectant Father, by George Schaefer (New York: Barnes and Noble, 1972).

The Father: His Role in Child Development, by D. Lynn (Monterey, CA: Brooks-Cole, 1974).

The Father's Almanac, by S. Adams Sullivan (Garden City, NY: Double-day, 1988).

The Father's Role: Applied Perspectives, edited by Michael Lamb (New York: John Wiley, 1986).

The Fathers' Book: Shared Experiences, edited by Carol Kort and Ronnie Friedland (Boston: G. K. Hall, 1986).

How to Be a Pregnant Father, by Peter Mayle (Secaucus, NJ: Lyle Stewart, 1977).

How to Father, by Fitzhugh Dodson (New York: New American Library, 1974).

The Liberated Man, by Warren Farrell (New York: Random House, 1975).

The Maternity Sourcebook: 230 Basic Decisions for Pregnancy, Birth and Baby Care, by Matthew and Wendy Lesko (New York: Warner Books, 1984).

New Father Survival Guide, by Larry Snydal and Carl Jones (New York: Franklin Watts, 1987).

Reassessing Fatherhood: New Observations on Fathers and the Modern Family, edited by Charlie Lewis and Margaret O'Brien (Newbury Park, CA: Sage, 1987).

The Role of the Father in Child Development, by M. Lamb (New York: John Wiley, 1976).

Who Will Raise the Children? New Options for Fathers (and Mothers), by James A. Levine (Philadelphia: Lippincott, 1976).

PREPARING FOR PARENTHOOD

A Baby? . . . Maybe, by Elizabeth M. Whelan, Sc.D. (New York: Bobbs-Merrill, 1976).

Letters to a Child Never Born, by Oriana Fallaci (New York: Doubleday, 1976).

Planning Ahead for Pregnancy: Dr. Cherry's Guide to Health, Fitness and Fertility, by Sheldon H. Cherry M.D. (New York: Viking, 1987).

LIFE IN THE WOMB

A Child Is Born, by Lennart Nilsson (New York: Dell, 1976).

The First Nine Months of Life, by Geraldine Lux Flanagan (New York: Simon & Schuster, 1962).

The Secret Life of the Unborn Child, by Thomas Verny (New York: Summit, 1981).

HAVING BABIES LATER IN LIFE

Having a Baby After 30, by Elisabeth Bing and Libby Colman (New York: Bantam, 1975).

Parents After Thirty, by Murray Kappelman and Paul Ackerman (New York: Wideview Books, 1981).

The Pregnancy After 30 Workbook, by Gail Brewer (Emmaus, PA: Rodale Press, 1978).
Pregnancy After 35, by Carole McCauley (New York: Pocket Books, 1976).

NUTRITION IN PREGNANCY

Eating Right: Before, During and After Pregnancy, by Elizabeth Whelan (New York: American Baby Books, 1982).
Nourishing Your Unborn Child: Nutrition and Natural Foods in Pregnancy, by Phyllis Williams (New York: Avon, 1975).

ADULT NEEDS IN PREGNANCY AND PARENTING

Making Love During Pregnancy, by Elisabeth Bing and Libby Colman (New York: Bantam, 1977).
The Private Life of Parents: How to Take Care of Yourself and Your Partner While Raising Happy, Healthy Children—A Complete Survival Guide, by Roberta Plutzik and Maria Laghi (New York: Everest House, 1983).
Sex, by Michael Carrera (New York: Crown Publishers, 1981).

BIRTH PLAN ALTERNATIVES

Birth Without Violence, by Frederick Leboyer (New York: Knopf, 1980).
The Complete Book of Midwifery, by Barbara Brennan and Joan Rattner Heilman (New York: E.P. Dutton, 1979).
The Rights of the Pregnant Patient: How to Have an Easier, Healthier Hospital Birth Together, by Valmai Howe Elkins (New York: Two Continents Publishing Group, 1976).
Shared Childbirth: A Guide to Family Birth Centers, by Philip Sumner and Celeste Phillips (St. Louis: C. V. Mosby, 1982)

CHILDBIRTH METHODS

Awake and Aware: Participating in Childbirth Through Psychoprophylaxis, by Irwin Chabon (New York: Delacorte, 1974).
Childbirth Without Fear, by Dr. Grantly Dick-Read (New York: Harper & Row, 1959).
The Complete Book of Pregnancy and Childbirth, by Sheila Kitzinger (New York: Knopf, 1980).
A Husband-Coached Childbirth, by Dr. Robert Bradley (New York: Harper & Row, 1974).
Methods of Childbirth, by Constance Bean (New York: Dolphin Books, 1982).
Prepared Childbirth, by Tarvez Tucker (New Canaan, CT: Tobey Publishing Company, 1975).

Six Practical Lessons for an Easier Childbirth, by Elisabeth Bing (New York: Bantam, 1969).
Thank You, Dr. Lamaze, by Marjorie Karmel (New York: Dolphin Books, 1965).

CESAREAN BIRTH

Cesarean Childbirth, by Christine Coleman Wilson and Wendy Roe (New York: Signet, 1980).
Cesarean Birth Experience, by Bonnie Donovan (Boston: Beacon, 1977).
Silent Knife, by Nancy Wainer Cohen and Lois Estner (South Hadley, MA: J.F. Bergen Publishers, 1983).

PREMATURE BIRTH

Born Early, by Dr. Mary Ellen Avery and Georgia Litwack (Boston: Little Brown, 1983).
Premature Babies: A Handbook for Parents, by Sherri Nance (New York: Arbor House, 1982).

BABY'S GROWTH AND DEVELOPMENT

Babyhood, by Penelope Leach (New York: Knopf, 1983).
Behavioral Individuality in Early Childhood, by T. A. Chess, H. G. Birch and M. E. Hertzig (New York: New York University Press, 1964).
The Biology of Dreaming, by Ernest Hartmann, M.D. (Springfield, IL: Charles C. Thomas, 1967).
Child Development and Socialization, by Jere E. Brophy (Chicago: Science Research Associates, 1977).
The Construction of Reality in the Child, by J. Piaget (New York: Basic Books, 1954).
The Development of the Infant and Young Child, by R. S. Illingworth (Baltimore: Williams & Wilkins, 1970).
The First Twelve Months of Life: Your Baby's Growth Month by Month, edited by Frank Caplan (New York: Bantam, 1973).
The Growth and Development of the Prematurely Born Infant, by C. M. Drillen (Baltimore: Williams & Wilkins, 1964).
The Growth of the Child, by Jerome Kagan (New York: W. W. Norton, 1978).
Infants and Mothers: Differences in Development, by T. Berry Brazelton, M.D. (New York: Dell, 1983).
The Magic Years: Understanding and Handling the Problems of Early Childhood, by Selma H. Fraiberg (New York: Scribner, 1959).
The Nature of the Child, by Jerome Kagan (New York: Basic Books, 1984).
New Parenthood: The First Six Weeks, by Cecilia Worth with Anna Marie Brooks (New York: McGraw-Hill, 1985).

The Nightmare, by Ernest Hartmann, M.D. (New York: Basic Books, 1984).

The Second Twelve Months of Life: Your Baby's Growth Month by Month, by Frank and Teresa Caplan (New York: Bantam, 1977).

Toddlers and Parents: A Declaration of Independence, by T. Berry Brazelton, M.D. (New York: Delacorte, 1974).

What Is This Thing Called Sleep?, by Hoskisson J. Bradley (London: David Poynter, 1976).

Your Baby and Child: From Birth to Age Five, by Penelope Leach (New York: Knopf, 1983).

CHILD BEHAVIOR AND PSYCHOLOGY

Attachment, Attachment and Loss Series, Vol. I, by J. Bowlby (New York: Basic Books, 1969).

Basic Sleep Mechanisms, O. Petre-Quadens and J. B. Schlag, eds. (London: Academic Press, 1974).

Behavior Problems of Normal Children, by J. W. Macfarlane, L. Allen and M. P. Honzik (Berkeley, CA: University of California Press, 1954).

The Causes, Controls and Organization of Behavior in the Neonate, by P. Wolff (New York: International Universities Press, 1965).

Change and Continuity in Infancy, by J. Kagan et al. (New York: John Wiley, 1971).

The Developmental Psychology of Jean Piaget, by J. H. Flavell (Princeton, NJ: Van Nostrand, 1963).

The Difficult Child, by Stanley Turecki, M.D., and Leslie Tonner (New York: Bantam, 1985).

Human Security: Some Reflections, by W. E. Blatz (Toronto: University of Toronto Press, 1966).

Mister Rogers Talks With Parents, by Fred Rogers and Barry Head (New York: Berkley, 1983).

Mother Care/Other Care, by Sandra Scarr (New York: Basic Books, 1984).

On Becoming a Family, by T. Berry Brazelton (New York: Delacorte Press/Lawrence, 1981).

Picking the Perfect Nanny: A Foolproof Guide to the Best At-Home Childcare, by Jane P. Metzroth (New York: Pocket Books, 1986).

Play, Dreams and Imitation in Childhood, by J. Piaget (New York: Norton, 1962).

The Roots of Individuality, by S. K. Escalona (Chicago: Aldine, 1968).

Separation: Anger and Anxiety, Attachment and Loss Series, Vol. II, by J. Bowlby (New York: Basic Books, 1973).

Temperament and Development, by A. Thomas and S. Chess (New York: Brunner/Mazel, 1977).

Toddler Taming: A Survival Guide for Parents, by Dr. Christopher Green (New York: Fawcett Columbine, 1984).

CHILD CARE, HEALTH & SAFETY

Baby and Child Care, Revised Edition, by Dr. Benjamin Spock (New York: Pocket Books, 1976).

Child Safety Is No Accident, by Jay M. Arena, M.D. (New York: Berkley Books, 1987).

The Child Care Encyclopedia, by Penelope Leach (New York: Knopf, 1984).

The Childwise Catalog: A Consumer Guide to Buying the Safest and Best Products for Your Children, by Jack Gillis and Mary Ellen R. Fise (New York: Pocket Books, 1986).

The Complete Mothercare Manual, Rosalind Y. Ting, M.D., Herbert Brant, M.D., and Kenneth S. Holt, M.D., consultants (New York: Prentice Hall, 1987)

Dr. Heimlich's Home Guide to Emergency Medical Situations, by Henry J. Heimlich, M.D. (New York: Simon & Schuster, 1980).

Emergency Baby First Aid: Newborn to Age Three, by Clifford L. Rubin, M.D., F.A.A.P. (New York: Berkley Books, 1980).

The Family Book of Child Care, by Niles Newton, Ph.D. (New York: Harper & Row, 1957).

Is My Baby All Right? A Guide to Birth Defects, by Virginia Apgar, M.D., M.P.H., and Joan Beck (New York: Trident Press, 1972).

Standard First Aid & Personal Safety, 2nd Ed., by the American Red Cross (Garden City, NY: Doubleday & Co., 1979).

Total Child Care: From Birth to Age Five, by Lorisa and Robert DeLorenzo (Garden City, NY: Doubleday & Co., 1982).

FREE PUBLICATIONS

"Keeping Danger Out of Reach,"
   Public Relations Dept.,
   Aetna Life & Casualty,
   151 Farmington Avenue,
   Hartford, Connecticut 06115.

"A Handbook of Child Safety" and "Guidelines—Child Safety,"
   Gerber Products Company,
   445 State Street,
   Fremont, Michigan 49412,
   Attention: Medical Marketing Service.

"Guide for the First-Time Baby Sitter," "Baby Care Basics,"
"Common Sense Care for Baby's Tender Skin,"
   Consumer and Professional Services,
   Johnson & Johnson Baby Products Company,
   Grandview Road,
   Skillman, New Jersey 08558.

"Personal Health Record," "Your Child's Health Care," "Immunizations: When & Why," "Fire Safety," "First Aid for the Family," "Planning for Safety," "Emergency Medical Card," "Dental Care: Questions and Answers," "Child Safety," and "Health and Safety Educational Materials Catalog,"
Metropolitan Life Insurance Company,
One Madison Avenue,
New York, New York 10010.

Index

Health maintenance organization.
    See HMO
Hearing, 88
Heartburn, 12
Heart massage, 206–207
Heatstroke, 204–205
Heimlich maneuver, 210
Hemophilus Influenza Type B
    Vaccine. *See* HIB vaccine
Hemorrhoids, 13
HIB vaccine, 185
HMO, 33–34
Holidays, as disruption to schedule,
    146
Home safety, 94, 102
Hospitals, 22
    procedures after birth, 48
Household monsters, 177–178
Housework, 19, 20
Hugging. *See* Cuddling
Humor, baby's sense of, 100
Husband-coached childbirth, 24–25
Hypersensitivity to stimulation,
    128–130

Illness, as disruption to schedule,
    146
Imagery relaxation, 44
Imagination, in dealing with
    anxieties, 172–173
Immunizations, 185
Inclement weather activities, 144
Indigestion, 12
Infections
    ear, 190
    mouth, 193
    urinary, 196–197
Insect bites, 201
Insurance, 32–33
Intravenous needle, 26

Jaundice, 50
Jealousy, 63–64
Jittery babies, 128–130
Jumping, 94–95, 103

Kitzinger, Sheila, 24

Labeling as a response to
    unacceptable behavior,
    167–169
Labor and childbirth, 46
    centers, 22–23
    cesarean, 42
    education, 24–25
    fathers during, 20–21, 39–41
    first stage, 37–38

active phase, 38, 43–44
    conversational phase, 38, 43
    transition, 44–45
    inducing, 43
    medical procedures during, 26
    methods, 24–25
    onset of, 37
    plan, 19, 21–22, 23
    second stage, 38–39
    pushing, 38–39, 45
    third stage, 39
Lamaze method, 24–25
Large motor control, 77–78, 80–81,
    112–113, 218
Large muscle control. *See* Large
    motor control; specific body
    parts
Laryngitis, 192
Left-handedness, 112
Legs
    fractures, 211
    learning to control, 86, 95
Length for age, 214–215
Lungs, common complaints of,
    193–195

Manipulative tantrum, 168–169
Massage during labor, 40, 41
Maturation level of the toddler,
    152–154
Meals
    preparation of, 9–10
    strategies for, 145
Medical complaints, common,
    188–198
Medicine, administering, 188
Midwife. *See* Certified nurse-midwife
Milk, 137
Miscarriage, 6, 15
Mobile, curtain rod, 87
Monsters, 177–178
Moods, 8, 14–15
    parent's, as cause of unacceptable
        behavior, 166–167
Morning sickness, 7–8, 14
Moro (startle) reflex, 85, 128, 172
Motion sickness, 198
Mouth
    infections, 193
    injuries, 202–203
    ulcers, 193
Muscle cramps, 13
Museums, 144

Naming the baby, 31
Nap schedule, 141–143. *See also*
    Sleeping